Before we get started, I should pᵢ
moment to thank the people who
possible, given me support or tolᶜ   ...ᵤᴋ ıt
up when I needed it, joined me on the journey
and allowed me to rabbit on, you know who you
are, so thank you.

A special thanks to my Son Jack for the morning
ritual of a "Luv U" text.

To Glen Jordan and Eddie Howe, two better
friends you could not hope to have.

To Steve Drew for going all over the country
with me back in the day, for contributing to this
book and for doing the spreadsheets!

To Natalie Rosato, Sarah Dineen and Everton
Stuart for their valuable contributions to this book

To Paul Anslow for continually reminding me to
stick to what I'm best at.

And of course, the irrepressible Nicola Ann for
keeping me in line, for ignoring me when I was
irritable and for knowing that feeding me is
always a good answer...

Chapter 1

As someone who's been in the industry for quite some time I very often get asked for tips and tricks of the trade, so I thought I'd throw it all together in a book.

I have a couple of reasons for writing this book. Firstly, it's ten years since I wrote 'The Telesales Handbook' (if you read it, then firstly, thank you and secondly, you'll probably have a feel for how I write) And secondly, writing a book is a great test of what you think you know.

I don't expect a Pulitzer Prize to be in the post any time soon but hopefully what I write makes some sense, is fun and is easy to read.

Another reason for putting this book together is because the call centre and telesales industry is a very misunderstood industry, we don't have the best reputation in business. So, if by writing this I can convince some people that actually we're just normal people trying to make a living and that the job can actually be a bit on the tough side on occasion then that'd be great.

I actually got into the industry a little by mistake.

When I first left school I actually went into the printing industry as a YTS trainee (That's Youth Training Scheme to the younger ones amongst us – I still have my first every pay slip…a massive £26.25) and then after years of people telling me, and I quote "With a gob like yours you should be in sales" I figured, what they hell, "better to have tried and failed then never try" or something equally philosophical.

To start with, I was fairly certain that nobody in their right mind was going to give someone with no experience a nice new company car and send me off to sell their wares. So I looked for an easier way in.

So my plan was to start with a job selling on the phone and then move into 'proper' sales when I'd got some experience.

I personally started my career on the telephone many years ago, making calls for a company that sold mobility products. They would advertise in the Sunday magazines and then when people called in to ask for a brochure we would say, "rather than send you a brochure I could arrange a free demonstration for you…" or something along those lines and we would then book a demo for them with one of the field reps. Those that didn't book would get a brochure and a follow up call a few days later to attempt to book them again and so it went on

Agreed, not exactly rocket science but we've all got to earn a living haven't we.

Now we were actually part of a bigger company, but our team specialised in walk in baths and that kind of thing. A few others came and went but there were four of us originally. Myself and Tors on the phone booking appointments. Hazel handling customer service and appointments for the fitters and Pete the boss.

Pete was the kind of boss who just let you get on with things. He was also the kind of boss that would order in a full English for us on a Friday morning!!

Hazel on the other hand was a law unto herself.

I have, on more occasions than I care to remember been witness to Hazel rocking up to the office having not yet gone to bed from a night out and consequently sleeping at her desk. I have actually seen her turn her back on Pete, hold paperwork in front of her face and merrily snooze away…really quite impressive with the boss sat six foot away!!

There are plenty of other Hazel stories I could tell you but I don't want to scare any small children…

Oh go on then just one quick one…

Pete the boss phones the office to speak to her and as she's not made it in yet so we tell him that she's in the loo, OK he says, I'll phone back in a bit.

Half an hour later he phones back and she's still not made it so we tell him she's still in the loo.

"Hope she's OK" comes the reply.

When a further half hour passes and Pete arrives at the office, Hazel has thankfully arrived, quite literally 2 minutes before him and not giving us time to give her the heads up about what we'd told him, he goes straight over to her and says. "Are you OK love, the lads told me how your morning started, you're obviously not well, you go on home"

"OK" she replies, giving us a rather confused look as she heads for the door!!

Some people have all the luck.

I feel I should tell you that this was a long time ago and that Hazel is now much more sensible and mother to a lovely little boy called Jacob (well, I say lovely, he and Jack once started a Nerf gun war in my house!)

As for Tors, a nice guy and great at what he was doing. He and I used to debate all sorts of things (and we may have played the odd game of Backgammon across the desk but I'm admitting to nothing) in between calls.

Another thing we used to do to make the day go by was to persuade my now ex-wife when she was at home, to cook us food and bring it over.

Many a happy afternoon spent scoffing Chilli Con Carne on jacket potatoes and similar delights.

Not what you'd call the most professional start to a career.

Now remember, I'd gone into telesales as a means to an end. But it turned out that not only did I enjoy it, but I was actually pretty good at it.

And so began my career…

I then moved to a large outsourcer and spent time there seeing how the big boys did it.

This was back in the days when Diallers were still quite new and we very often spent more time in the car park waiting for it to be fixed rather than actually making any calls.

The real fun with diallers back then was when your screen popped up with the next call and no name appeared (it was supposed to pop up automatically in time for you to see who you were calling)

Many a "Hello Sir/Madam.." used in those instances.

When you are changing campaigns from day to day, you learn to be adaptable very quickly. You also learn to have notes in front of you so that you don't forget who you're talking to, what you're talking about etc.

I actually managed to get my first taste of being a Team Leader during my time there, so I got to have my first dabble with management and started to see my career take shape.

As an outsourcer we would regularly have new campaigns to work on and these would always involve some degree of training from the client.

The reason I mention this is because we were already doing a campaign for Lloyds TSB selling accident protection and they wanted to add a further product – Accidental Death protection.

Agreed, not the most exciting of topics. 100 plus calls a day starting with "Have you thought about what would happen if you were to die unexpectedly"?

They select a bunch of us to start the campaign off with yours truly being one of the chosen few. I'll apologise now for not being able to remember the name of the nice lady they sent to educate us, but we had a couple of days of product stuff and then it was on to the script.

As we were using a dialler the script was on screen and took a form similar to a flow chart. The question for you to ask would pop up on the screen and you'd have a yes or no box to click to get to the next question and so on.

There was only one slight issue I had with this and that was the first question we were supposed to ask.

Let me explain. We all know that to get the bigger payouts on these types of insurances then the situations and conditions are pretty specific, but telling prospective customers that in the first few seconds is unlikely to go in your favour.

With me being younger and slightly more impetuous back then, I stick my hand up and voice my concern.

Credit where it's due the Lloyds trainer got my point and we all played around with the script to get something we could work with. Something that was a little less, upfront, shall we say.

We went live with it that evening and thankfully it worked a treat – large sigh of relief from me as I would've looked very silly had it not worked – it was here that I started to think that maybe I have an ability to notice a problem and come up with a solution and an interest in coaching/training.

The downside in working for a fairly large company can be that you risk staying in a position until the one above you opens up and that can be quite a while.

As my plan was to build a career, I then decided to look for my next upwards move.

Next step for me was I became a Sales Account Manager for an office supplies company, with a mixture of cold calling and account management. I learnt a few tricks there, not least the fact that sales don't just happen, there's actually some effort involved!

My mistake was to not to have a good month of sales, that's obviously a good thing, where I went wrong was thinking I'd cracked it and now my customers would just phone me with their order and I could relax.

Yeah, unfortunately that's not quite how it works!

I learnt that not only do you have to keep in contact with your customers, so that they stay as your customers, but you have to keep finding new ones as well.

Who knew…

Needless to say, I very quickly changed my approach, much to the relief of the boss Mark.

Now back then Mark was a rather excitable chap – although he has mellowed somewhat now – and kept up a constant barrage of…

"How are the orders"?
"How are we doing today"?
"Why aren't you on the phone"?
and so on.

Now I didn't really mind this, he was only thinking about his business after all.

But we did manage to get our own back now and again.

I remember one occasion. Mark had this habit (I think he called it motivation!) of telling us that one day we might be good enough at sales to 'hold his coat'

Credit where it's due, he built his business up to £700,000 turnover and started it by buying a van and knocking on doors.

So anyway, back to 'holding coats'

One morning Mark walks into the office and says to me.

"Well done Stu, we've just had an order in from (can't remember the name) in Avonmouth, so that's another new customer for you. I tried to get them on board for years and couldn't, so good job"

With that, I stand up, walk over to the coat rack, grab my coat and holding it out towards Mark I say…

"You'll be wanting this then"

Much laughter followed.

One of the reasons we differed from most of the other office supplies companies – and there were quite a few back then – was that we had a retail shop attached to the business.

What it also meant was if a customer phoned us and said "I need it asap" we would pop downstairs, 'borrow' it from the shelf and then get it delivered.

It was great for us on the commercial side but poor Piers the shop manager suffered untold grey hairs when doing stock takes!!

The other huge benefit for us was the location of the office. We were perfectly placed at one end of a pedestrian crossing, the opposite end being taken by a lovely big Asda with a café that served a rather splendid full English breakfast!

To make it even more fabulous we got to know the ladies who worked there which generally got us extra helpings – and for that I am eternally grateful, many a cold morning improved with one of those breakfasts!!

I was of course, deeply upset to discover they'd turned the café into a MacDonald's!!

I still catch up with Mark when I'm out and about. His middle daughter, who was in school uniform when I worked for him is now CEO of a recruitment company and his youngest is owner/Head Chef at her own restaurant.

Now as I said, this was career move for me, so from there came my first move into a management role as a Telesales and Marketing Manager – an interview that lasted about five hours for a job I didn't think I would get!

I will at this point offer my sincerest thanks to the owner and boss at Aquatec, Sue Baker-Joy, who gave me the above job and a lady I still refer to as boss (old habits etc). A lovely lady who I spent more time with than my wife, purely because we worked 10 to 12 hour days through the week and most weekends. So much so that when we we're working the phones together, words were fairly unnecessary because we knew each other so well.

Her son actually has the same birthday as me (although depressingly he's a lot younger!!).

When I took over the team it stood at about a dozen telesales appointment setters feeding two reps. The reps – Steve and Steve – had to go on appointments set by the team to demonstrate, in peoples homes, water softeners. So not the easiest sell I can assure you, but the guys managed it and both Steve's sold pretty well into the bargain.

I could tell you some horror stories about water quality, but these days a quick google search will do the same if you're that way inclined.

Although I gather my knowledge of water quality etc did benefit my then Step-daughter and allow her to 'show off' in a science class.

Now you have to remember that, as I mentioned, this was a job I didn't think I'd get. Purely because I had not one single bit of management training or anything even closely resembling that. So when I took over this team I quite frankly had no clue what I was going to do and was very much a 'duck out of water'.

The team actually built to around the mid-twenties in number by the time I'd finished with half a dozen reps.

At this point I should mention some of the team who made my life fun and gave me grey hairs at the same time.

Anyone who's ever done any kind of 'telesales training' has no doubt heard the phrase 'smile while you dial' a little on the cheesy side but it does actually work.

I have only seen the opposite used to great effect once in my career, by Angela McQuade, lovely as she was and my right-hand woman for a while, she was the most deadpan person on the phone I have ever heard, but contrary to popular belief was actually quite successful on the phone. I put it down to the fact that she just didn't take no for an answer.

The conversation would go something like this.

Prospect "Could I say no this time"

Angela "Yes of course, now as I was saying…"

Delivered in a completely deadpan voice but still professional and polite and low and behold an appointment would be booked.

It goes against everything sales people are taught, but it worked, so far be it for me to argue. In fact, she once said to me that if you asked her friends to describe her in one word they would say 'dull'. I also hold her responsible for my Son Jack being born as it was after a night out with her that the discussion of having children started between myself and his Mum.

Then you've got Natalie, generally considered by the others as the best in the team and her daughter Nicole would raid my desk for sweets and chocolate whenever she could.

Natalie is what these days I would call a solid performer. Always did well and never gave me much to moan about. We had the odd cross word over the couple of years I was Manager, but it all came out in the wash.

Then you had Laura who worked in Ibiza during the summer months, Chris who was one of the few lads on the team when I took over and numerous others.

Gemma, for example, she was always very straight with the people around her. If she didn't like you, she just didn't talk to you, not many grey areas with Gemma – I have to add that she is now a mother of two boys and a little more forgiving…I think.

But just to balance the odds I believe that at the first Christmas party it was Gemma who started the 'down in one or show us your bum' drinking game. A game that left a few people very much the worse for wear next morning.

Something else that took place at the party was the visit by Joel's rather excitable girlfriend. Joel was one of the guys on the team and I think it fair to say was considered a bit smooth.

Here's the scenario. Said girlfriend calls Joel's mobile and says meet me in the foyer now, so off he trots. What is unknown to both is that some of the girls are already in reception getting some fresh air before commencing with more merriment – something they did rather well.

So as the, rather heated, conversation between Joel and his young lady reaches it's predictable conclusion – and by that I mean Joel's girlfriend accusing him of sleeping with someone else – Joel defends himself with the phrase.

"You're just being stupid"

Good plan mate, tell the irate woman who's mad at you that you think she's stupid!!

Which results in Joel getting a slap round the face, heard from the other side of the room.

In an instant, Natalie, who has until now been standing by just listening, decides that this isn't on and she should defends Joels' honour by promptly returning the favour on Joels' behalf much to the young ladys surprise then merrily turns around and goes back to the bar to carry on drinking, leaving Joel unsure as to his next move.

These guys (or to be precise, mainly girls) were a big part of my life for a good couple of years. We worked hard and when the opportunity presented itself, we played hard.

I remember one work night out -arranged as a thank you for a brilliant first quarter, which started with a meal at a Wetherspoons on Bristol waterfront – which kept two members of staff busy the whole time just bringing the drinks!!

Since starting my consultancy, I have been back and worked for Sue on a couple of occasions, but that's a whole different story.

It was at this point that I started to think about working for myself.

When you've been working in an industry for any length of time, people get to know you and what you're capable of. With that in mind there were a few occasions when I was asked by other telesales and call centre operations to "Come and do some training for us".

Now I didn't mind this, it was fun, it honed my skills and I got paid.

The turning point for me was watching a freelance trainer deliver a course full to overflowing of the kind of stuff I was teaching my guys day in and day out but making as much in a day as I was making working six days a week!

I'm not particularly shallow, alright maybe a little bit, but add to that the fact that my wife was pregnant and not having much fun and we had some money saved up I took the plunge and handed in my notice.

Now I was working for myself and so came the launch into consulting and a few years of headaches, proposals, networking and spinning several plates at once.

Since that time I have helped a first division football club increase season ticket sales, a national accident management company train a couple of hundred new staff, written a telephone selling skills course (a course that I was asked not to call a sales course!), doubled the sales of an outsourcer using the same amount of staff and numerous other set ups, training sessions and improvements to established teams and written a book.

I suppose the best way to describe what I do is to use the statement used by my mother when asked what I do for a living - "If you have a call centre and you want it to do better he can help you and if you want to have your own call centre he can make it for you" – laymans terms, but it pretty much covers it.

My Son Jack was asked by his teacher, when he was about 5 years old, what he wanted to be when he grew up. Fairly standard and the sort of thing we've all been asked when at that age. Jack responds with "I want to be like Daddy". And what does your Daddy do? She asks. He pauses for a moment and then replies with "My Daddy makes people on the phone be better" apparently said with a huge beaming smile on his face.

A long-time friend of mine jokes that I can be "dropped in any town in the UK and as long as I have my mobile phone I can create a call centre" a grand claim I'll agree, but probably not too far from the truth, if you work in any industry for long enough you will gain the contacts you need.

If you've ever stood in the middle of a buzzing call centre you'll know exactly what I mean (especially if you're the one responsible for it!!) and those of you who haven't just don't know what you're missing!

Add to this the people who work in the call

centres, a mix of people of all shapes and sizes, cultures, opinions and personalities it's either a huge can of worms waiting to be opened or a great place to flourish I can't always decide.

At the last count the industry employed something like 9% of the country's workforce and yet we are probably one of the least understood and least respected industries, but the fact remains, many businesses today have realised that the telephone, used properly, is a very cost-effective selling tool.

OK, let's look at some of those tips I talked about.

I used these a while ago as the basis of a training session, so I thought I'd use them as a good place to start. I'll throw in some technical stuff interspersed with as many stories as I can remember – where I will no doubt embarrass myself as much as anyone else!

Just to show that I am by no means infallible when it comes to my behaviour in the call centre (which will become even more obvious as you read through this book) I remember at the beginning of my career as a consultant, working as the Interim Operational Manager for an outsourcer in Melksham, who at the time were selling subscriptions to local newspapers on behalf of several media groups.

What this meant was that every time someone got a sale (or more precisely, the agreement to take the relevant paper) we had to confirm the order.

Therefore, we had half a dozen people walking the floor ready to jump in and confirm as soon as they could.

On occasion, we'd get really busy so it was all hands on deck, which included me.

I'm sat at my desk with the office door open and I hear the cry "OP" as in Order Processor (just to clarify, that's what the guys called out when the needed an order confirmed – with the customer on hold I hasten to add!!). When I hear it for the third time, I jump up and go to confirm it myself.

I grab the headset from the agent and start going through the confirmation script. As I'm in full flow, I casually sit down in the agents chair, without thinking I tuck my leg under myself as I sit.

A confirmation normally took a couple of minutes, but on this occasion, because the customer had loads of questions, it actually took more like ten minutes. That in itself is fine, if the customer had questions, I'm happy to answer them.

The unfortunate thing here is that for the whole time, I'm sat, effectively, on my left leg.

So, call wrapped up, I go to stand, left leg numb, doesn't support me and so down I go on full display to a 48 seat call centre. Just, I might add, as the MD walks out of his office to speak to me.

Of course, I just went with it and giggled my arse off!!

There are more stories I'll tell you from that call centre, but I'll get to those later.

OK, so back to the tips I mentioned.

Chapter 2

It only works if you do it properly...

This may sound silly but far too many people make a half-hearted attempt at call centres, telesales or telemarketing and then wonder why it doesn't work.

You would not believe how many people think that working in a call centre is easy. As with anything else, if you approach it in a professional and prepared way you stand a much better chance of success.

I have, over the years, been asked on numerous occasions to help in the set up of call centres and telesales teams and every time without fail it is one of the hardest things to do smoothly and without drama.

I remember the first one I had to do. It was for a 16 seat operation that had to be put into what can only be described as a junk room.

It was one of those rooms that large businesses often have, the kind of room that when you can't find the right place for something, you dump it in there. Or when you order new things you file the old ones in there.

When I first saw it there was actually half a conservatory window in the corner (that's not a hint at the type of business by the way, it was apparently left over from a show!)

The idea was this, at the time they had two separate teams of eight, one team was spread across the Bristol office and the other was up in Cheshire.

I had to firstly assess the process and performance of the Cheshire based team which was due to close down (never a fun thing to be involved in) whilst also setting up and recruiting for the South West office.

Now let me remind you about the junk room where I'm supposed to set up this new, sparkling call centre.

Not only does it include half a conservatory

window alongside several broken chairs, tables, computers it has windows that have grills across them and don't open more than an inch or two!

So, when I get back from the Cheshire office I start the recruitment process to fill the brand new South West office. Now anyone who's met me or worked with me will know I am not the biggest fan of recruitment, it drives me insane.

In fact, in regards to this set up I have to give huge thanks and undying love to Emma Copping at Brook Street for doing it all for me.

I've learnt over the years to always line up more interviews etc than you actually need and if you're recruiting for, let's say ten people, it pays to actually recruit for twelve because you will always lose a couple in the first few days and weeks therefore leaving you with what you originally wanted.

Before I start ranting too much about recruitment (although I may start again later) let me just say that I was given 28 days to turn the junk room into an operational call centre and I did in 24 but please hold your applause until the end – if you know what you're doing and you plan for everything you know will happen then it becomes a little easier, not easy, just easier.

All of guys that have done any work for me will no doubt agree that we've all heard these phrases before.

"It's all set up properly so why isn't it doing what we need it to"? or "We did everything right so why aren't they performing"?

And nine times out of ten it's something really simple or obvious that's stopping them getting what they want!

Setting up a call centre or telesales team is actually very involved if it's done properly.

Oddly enough it's not as easy as just sticking a bunch of people in a room with desks and phones and then crossing your fingers – although my life would be an awful lot easier if it was!

A point proved quite simply by the fact that my other book, The Telesales Handbook, is written with that exact process in mind and took

approximately three months to complete (and for me to make sure I hadn't missed anything!)
I shan't bore you with the technicalities but I will throw in another story.

I was involved in the set up of a new Bristol call centre for HelpHire, the accident management company. Now my part didn't kick in right at the start, so I had some time to kill so I helped out wherever I could.

On the occasion in question I was playing at IT assistant (basically I carried the IT managers toolbox!). So there we are, setting up the switch for the call centre – hundreds of phone lines, CAT 5 cabling and I don't know what else.

IT manager says to me, "Hold this fibreglass cable still and be very careful with it".

Now the aforementioned fibreglass cable is protruding from what looks to me like a spaghetti junction of cables, so I say

"What happens if I drop it or break it"?

The casual response is…

"The whole switch goes down"

I have never in my life been so aware of how steady my hand needed to be!

I was also never more relieved to get back to the relative comfort of the training room!

There is also a tendancy to over complicate things when setting up a new call centre or telesales operation.

That may seem a little contradictory when you look at my previous statement about a set up being quite involved. But in my humble opinion, being involved and being complicated are not the same thing.

Let me give you an example.

Excel spreadsheets get used quite a lot in our industry and with the increased use of CRM systems over the last few years they are almost just a splash in the ocean.

But they're a good place to start if you want to get a fairly simple look at what's going on with your team.

Now if you were to ask myself and someone else (who shall remain nameless…Mr Drew) to create a spreadsheet to give you an outline of the teams performance my spreadsheet is very likely to be pretty simple and to the point, whereas the other is likely to be a little more complicated.

I should probably mention at this point that spreadsheets are on my ever increasing list of necessary evils and young Mr Drew is the one that normally does them when we've been onsite together because, although I am perfectly capable, he's far better at them than I am – my excuse is that as a highly experienced consultant I have learnt to delegate (although he may disagree slightly…)

I have no desire to keep harping on about "If you do it right in the first place…" because firstly, common sense dictates that this makes sense, but secondly, that's not entirely true,

Yes, of course, if you set something up properly initially then your chances of success will obviously increase.

But setting it up properly and running it properly are two entirely different things and sadly the latter is often overlooked.

On the subject of being over looked, I remember visiting one client who said to me – and I'm quoting this as precisely as I can.

"We've set everything up ready to have a 'kick-ass' telesales team, we just need you to train them"

"Excellent" I say, "So you've got the room ready"?

"Yep, all in place"

"Great, and you've recruited the staff"?

"Ah, no not yet…"

"OK, not to worry, perhaps that should be our first port of call"

"Yeah, probably a good idea"

"Why don't I pop over in a couple of days and we'll get the ball rolling and take a look at the whole thing"

"OK, great, thanks Stu"

So, two days later I rock up at the office and they lead me proudly to their sparkly new sales room and I immediately spot something amiss.

"Looks great, could I just ask one quick question"?

"Of course" came the proud reply

"What will they use to call people"?

"The telephones obviously..."

This last comment kind of trailed off as he turned to the room and noticed what I'd seen straight away – they hadn't put phones on the desks!!

They'd been so focussed on creating a great environment for their new team, that they'd forgotten the obvious.

An honest mistake and one that we now laugh about.

Although I feel I must add that creating a good environment for your staff is not something to be taken lightly.

Telesales can suffer from a bad reputation at the best of times so the more professional you act the quicker you will be able to overcome their fears. Long gone are the days where you can just take a stab at it and hope for the best.

These days, thankfully, there are rules and regulations, standards and boundaries. I think those of us in the industry will agree, it's been a long time coming but we're all very glad it's happened. As with any industry, the more professional you act the better you are seen by the people you want to have as customers.

Do your research and know why you're calling

If you're knee deep in a busy day, there's nothing worse than getting a call from someone asking for "The Proprietor" or "The person in charge of....", it just screams cold call and immediately puts people on the defensive, the walls will come flying up and it's never going to end how the caller would like.

If you add the standard "My name is…." and "How are you today"? then you're probably on a hiding to nothing.

On the other side of the coin, if you're the one making the call, if you don't know why you're calling how will you know when you've achieved your goal?

Think about, if you were the recipient, how would you like to have a call opened. Doing your research is really important to the success of your call.

Now, I'll agree, what I've just said is aimed mostly towards those amongst us doing outbound and sales calls but the same research issue does come up for those on the customer service and inbound side who find themselves having to make call backs to customers.

Knowing who you're supposed to be speaking to, why you need to speak to them and what's happened so far is firstly going to make the call go much easier and secondly, will make the customer feel much more confident that you're dealing with their problem.

Whether you're inbound or outbound, sales or customer service, the fact remains that if you do your research, you will act and sound much more professionally and life will be much easier – you can add knowing your product/service into the research heading as it's just as important.

Don't get me wrong, life on the phone will never be perfect, that's the nature of what we do, but doing your research and sounding professional will certainly make it easier!

Always measure what you do…and act on it

KPI's (Key Performance Indicators) or targets are basically there to help you measure your teams' performance, but you have to know how to read them, what they mean and how to act on the results.

We all know what KPI's are and why we should have them, but so many people have them almost as a comfort thing and never actually do anything with them.

Pick any CRM system you like and it will no doubt provide you with a performance report. But what does it actually tell you, do you interpret it properly and do you act on what you read?

Most people will take a look at the report and decide whether the results are above or below what they should be and then either breathe a sigh of relief if it's over or decide who to moan at if it's below.

I have been in far too many meetings where KPI reports were handed out and almost immediately tucked away into folders never again to see the light of day.

But a decent KPI sheet can tell you so much more.

For example, you have an agent who is making plenty of calls but not getting any sales – more than likely an agent who's not been on the phone long and is struggling to get past a certain point. Therefore, their Team Leader should be looking at further training or at the very least some coaching.

Or an agent who makes the calls and gets the sales but has a high cancellation rate – for me that gives me an instant worry that they're saying something they shouldn't have and the customer is finding out afterwards and consequently cancelling. My answer to that would be to listen in to their calls away from the team to see if you can see the area that's perhaps not so clear and then coach the agent to correct what they're saying.

When reading a KPI sheet you should be able to make observations about all team members included on it – good or bad – and then know what action to take following those observations.

There has often been a tendancy, when looking at a KPI sheet, to ignore an individual or individuals if the results are overall what is needed. This can lead to any number of other issues not least the moral of the team.

If you only have a portion of your team that is performing as expected and you ignore it because the team result is where it should be then you may have some hiccups further down the road.

People within the team will know who is and who isn't performing and the last thing you want is resentment brewing.

You must look at the individual, you cannot just take a KPI sheet or performance report that shows a successful week etc and ignore everything else.

That report will show you quite a lot of information about your team, how they're performing, how they're feeling and very possibly, what's going to happen next week.

Looking at the results for each person in turn will not only allow you to be aware of any peaks and troughs and obviously plan accordingly but it can also highlight any training needs.

When it comes to a KPI's sheet, it should be used for the purpose it has been designed. It is a report on the way your team and its members are performing both as a unit and individually.

It does not matter whether your team is sales or customer service, there will still be Key Performance Indicators that you need them to meet or exceed and the report you get on this information will give you many of the answers you need.

For a sales team the KPI's are generally based on the revenue targets whereas customer service or support teams are more than likely working on such KPI's as first call resolution etc.

Tenacity wins the day

The next call could be the yes – as I already mentioned, it's hard work, you have to be prepared to keep going even if you keep getting 'No's', remember every no brings you closer to a yes! I know I'm bit old school, but it's true!

Agreed this is more often than not something for the sales people amongst us but the same frame of mind can be utilised by anyone.

Do your job properly and keep at it and you will see the rewards.

Now before I get on my soap box about this, the tenacious approach of any team is a lot to do with the motivational skill of the manager and how well they can get behind their team and reward them when they do well.

Let me give you an example of how this can work.

In one call centre, there was a young lad named Jack, who was previously working in hotels. He asked me how he could be successful, my advice to him once he'd finished his induction was "Get your head down, do it how I show you to do it and make lots of phone calls and that'll give you a pretty good start"

OK, a bit blunt and I'll agree, there's a bit more to it than that but it was a simple starting point for a lad with no experience.

A lad who as it stands ended up as one of the top performers and beating people with far more experience – he also managed to get me to say yes to a pay rise on the back of it so he must have some fairly decent negotiation skills…

Remember, on the phone it's more about how you say something rather than what you say

Without wishing to state the obvious, one of the

biggest differences between face-to-face customer contact and dealing with them over the phone is that we can see their reactions/environment or the look on their face.

On the phone, all we have is what we hear them say and how we use our own voice. Your tone of voice, the pace of your voice and how you generally sound will have a big impact on how you are received by the person you are calling/speaking to.

Practice how to speak on the phone, it may sound silly, but it will pay dividends in the long term.

Think of it like this.

Remember me telling you about Angela and her deadpan voice. How do you think that was perceived by the person she was talking to?

What impression do you have of her?

If you heard that type of voice over the phone, how do you think she looks?

Whether we admit it or not we all judge people on

how they sound, if that's all we know of them.

Try this, you phone a customer service line and the person who answers talks in a high pitched, excitable voice.

Think about two things. Firstly, (people make assumptions that they're female) so what does she look like etc and secondly with such a voice how confident are you that your issue will be resolved?

My apologies to any ladies who talk in such a manner, I'm purely just trying to make a point. The reason I've brought this up is because I've delivered training sessions on this on a regular basis that spends a whole day on this topic and always brings a lot of discussion.

We've spent many an afternoon 'debating' the pros and cons of different voices.

The other thing that comes in to play with this is accents. Again, human nature makes us judge, or make presumptions if you like, about people based on how they sound and accents are not generally something that you can stop doing!

There's been lots of studies over the years about which accents are the most well received and the least well received.

Without wishing to open up a big old can of worms, some accents can give the person on the receiving end and immediate impression of who they're talking to.

I'm from Gloucester originally and some would say that with that 'farmer's accent I wouldn't come across as the most intelligent of folk.

Because of the job I've done for many years I have actually refined my accent to keep it fairly neutral – although when I'm tired the odd word does creep in and I did, after all live in Bristol for over 20 years!

I promise you it's not that I am at all embarrassed about the place I'm from, far from it, but when you do the job that I do you want to make sure that the person you're talking to is listening to what you're saying and not focussed somewhere else.

I remember when I was working in Melksham with the newspaper guys. There was a guy on the team called Albert.

Now Alberts parents were originally from Ghana so as you'd expect, Albert had a bit of an accent even though he was born and bred in the UK.

So there he is merrily chatting away to a lady on the phone. At the time I was walking the floor making sure everything was going to plan, but after couple of minutes I can see him getting a bit frustrated.

Because of this I casually wander over so that I can hear what's being said and help if necessary.

The short version of the story is that because of his accent the poor woman was convinced that she was talking to someone in a call centre in some foreign land. Albert in his efforts to convince her otherwise was slowly but surely describing everything he could see out of the window, quoting TV shows and in a last ditch attempt was reading to her from today's newspaper.

It wasn't until I got on the phone and spoke to her that she started to come around and to her credit she apologised to Albert whole heartedly.
It just goes to show what difference an accent can make and how people pre-judge.

Over the last few years some accents have become more accepted that they previously were. The most notable being the Geordie accent, largely I would guess thanks to the dulcet tones of a certain Cheryl and of course, Ant and Dec.

Of course, there are occasions when having the right accent can be a massive bonus.

I remember my very first project as a consultant. It was for Bristol City Football Club. With the start of the season fast approaching season ticket sales weren't what the club was hoping for so they decided to put together a telesales campaign to speak to their huge database of previous ticket holders and see if they could encourage them to buy again.

Enter yours truly with some words of wisdom and a couple of perfectly placed training sessions.

I was told that they'd tried this before with an outsourced company in, if I remember correctly, Nottingham. The problem had been that when people complained about, shall we say, parking near the club the guys in Nottingham could offer no help at all. So using a team made up of people working at the club and therefore knowing the area and of course sounding very much like Bristolians worked a treat.

I guess it's a case of picking your battles...

Chapter 3

Know your 'cost per seat'

And what it means in terms of sales. Cost Per Seat is very often seen as one of those anomalies that people either get or they don't.

It's one of the first questions we ask when talking to a new or prospective client and very often they're so caught up in everything else that they don't know it.

It's a really simple formula but it's massively important as a basic figure to work from.

OK, let's say your agent costs you £100 per day for him or her to come to work, every sale they make you get £25, so for you to be able to pay them, they must make 4 sales each day. Your own figures may be different, but the process is the same.

Now the costs of your agent should include their daily wage, call costs, utilities and anything else that they have to have in order to do their job.

Although it's a simple formula it's open to negotiation. I've used a small and fairly obvious figure in my example but although the 'cost' figure might be similar for your team how many sales they'll need for you to stop panicking will differ depending on what they sell and it's value.

For example, if a sale is worth £500 then, sticking with my £100 per agent example, they'd only need to make one sale a week to 'pay their way' although I'm sure you'd rather they did a bit more than that!

Giving staff and agents a beneficial and rewarding incentive scheme will always pay dividends

We all like to get rewarded for a job well done and when we do we work harder!

Once again this will be a massive help in motivating your team.

Keeping your team motivated is a constant struggle at the best of times, but when times are hard or work is a little low it becomes even harder.

Although we all understand that motivation is a must you don't need to break the bank to achieve it – as you'll see in a minute – but you do need to put some thought in to it.

There are a few things that you need to consider when deciding which route to take. First and foremost being how much money has the boss given you to spend!

Now there's no need to panic at this point, you don't necessarily need an absolute fortune to achieve great results – I have in the past motivated a team of 48 with an allowance of £50.00 per week. You have to appreciate that it's not about the money, it's about winning.

People, by their very nature, are generally competitive, and that's something you can use to your advantage.

Keep things fresh.

As obvious as it may sound, the key to motivation is to keep things fresh. Any job, however much you enjoy it, can become monotonous.

This is even truer for the call centre/telesales environment what with the added pressure of performing and hitting targets not usually associated with other jobs.

Small 'quick fix' prizes.

Monthly bonuses and incentive schemes are always good, but what will keep them motivated throughout the month is the small 'quick fix' stuff, the here and now, if you like.

The little prizes they can take away with them as soon as they win them (or hit target). I once started a game of pass the parcel using old newspapers and pound shop toys that not only lifted moral but also created a considerable increase in sales!

We've all played games such as Monopoly and Snakes and Ladders and depending on how much room you have in the office you can set these up and use them as a tool to push the team forward.

All you have to do is get hold of some pens and paper and have the 'board' set up on the walls and then you basically tell the team that for every sale they get a 'move' on the board and the winner gets whatever prize you deem suitable.

This will work for pretty much any board game, it's cheap to set up and you can add smaller prizes in if you wish – of course, you don't have to offer them prizes just for sales, you can work it with most of your KPI's depending on which ones need improving – think about the SLAs your customer service team are tasked to meet.

Now if you really want to get the blood flowing and have the room for it there's lots of things you can do.

I have previously set up a company Olympics whereby when they got a sale they had to complete a physical challenge.

Now because we had a mixed team of old and young, male and female, we had to make the challenges appropriate so there were challenges such as darts and Kerplunk for the more sedate amongst us and skipping etc for the more adventurous.

As a quick side note, one of the older ladies in the team, was, by her own admission, not very good at some of the 'events' but when it came to the darts day nobody could get near her!!

The end result was that everyone had a fair chance of winning and nobody felt left out. The overall winner was presented with a 'winners T-shirt' and runners up were given other prizes.

As another side note, Rosanne who won the first year told me that she wore the T shirt when she gave birth to her daughter. Information I could've done without by thanks anyway.

The great thing is this can now be rolled out every year.

Regular, effective and relevant training is massively important and a great motivator. If you want them to perform properly and consistently then you have to give them the tools to do so.

Training is always good, it keeps people up to date and focused on the job at hand, it keeps their skills at the forefront and it will show them that management are obviously interested in how well they do their job, etc.

If they are given good quality training that covers the topics and issues they are faced with then they will respond and to a certain extent motivate themselves to stick with what they learn.

Offer a nice clean working environment.

You need to make sure that the environment they are working in is conducive to good performance. Everyone likes to work somewhere nice, clean carpets, working computers and phones, a couple of nice plants etc.

Consider this, which team do you think would give the best performance, the one who works in a scruffy office where the equipment only works half of the time and the managers never offer any support, or the team that works in a clean, friendly office where everything works properly and managers spend their day patting you on the back?

I appreciate that I've given a simple example but the fact remains that if your office is clean and welcoming then your team will want to be there and motivation is much easier to come by.

One of the best things to do when organising any type of motivation is to keep a record of what you did and how well it went so that eventually you will have a book of motivational activities to call on as and when the team needs a boost.

We all like to be rewarded or praised for doing it well.

A good reward scheme is a great motivator, especially if your team are conducting outbound calls.

Human nature dictates that no matter what job we do, we all like to be rewarded or praised for doing it well. Sales people live by that, generally because the better they do the more money they get!

For the best results, what you have to do is have more than one programme running at any given time – immediate, daily, weekly, monthly – it doesn't really matter what time scales are involved – the key is to run a programme that suits all members of the team.

Basically, the thing that might motivate the top

Sales person won't necessarily work with an average performer and vice versa. If you have different options then you should be able to give all of them something to aim for.

What we must not forget amongst all these games etc is that there is no replacement for a good management style.

A pat on the back from a manager that you respect and trust is worth its weight in gold. We must also not forget that clean and suitable surroundings and a good training program are the stable diet of a well performing team.

The bottom line is this – manage your team properly, train them, support them, use what you have first, there is no need to spend fortunes and whatever you do make sure that everyone has a fair chance, otherwise you risk alienating some of your team and defeating the object of motivation.

Never underestimate the importance of ongoing coaching

I see too many managers who just leave their guys to get on with it after their induction. To get the best results you have to keep on top of their performance and that means ongoing coaching, sit next to them and listen to what they're saying and make constructive observations.

Notice that I said 'constructive', you can't just sit here and tell them what they did wrong – you have to make sure they understand it and help them to fix it. You need their buy in.

With any size team coaching should play an important part if you want it to succeed.

All of worlds the most successful teams, athletes and business people have gotten where they are by utilising the skills of a coach, so doesn't it make sense that if you want your sales or customer service team to perform at their best, then you need someone to help them achieve it?

To summarise, coaching is about helping someone perform a skill or solve a problem better that they would normally be able to.

It's about helping people to perform better than they currently do, to develop their skills over a period of time.

You encourage, you share knowledge and you adopt an open style to allow others to learn from you.

Coaching should be used across the board so that all team members benefit from it, whether they are new starters, experienced or just those that want to develop.

Of course, a good coach can also coach those more senior than them...assuming that they want to learn!

The benefits are different for an individual compared to those of a team.

For example, a person coached on a 1-2-1 basis will be able to learn at their own pace, have more involvement in the process and will not have to worry or be embarrassed about saying or asking the wrong thing.

Coaching a team as a whole will allow them to become clear about the goals it has to achieve, it can focus them all in the right direction and will generally raise the skill level of all involved.

There is of course, a gain for the coach as well if they do it properly. A good coach will develop closer relationships, they will discover new ways of helping people by listening to the feedback they get and by seeing the people they coach grow.

And let's not forget the gain for the business.

Improving the ability and performance of your people will add value to your bottom line. There is a time and place for coaching, what I mean is that there are times when you shouldn't coach but rather wait until afterwards and then coach.

For example, if the team are up against a deadline. You should help where you can but leave the coaching stuff till calm has landed and you can discuss with the team to prepare them for next time.

We can, as you'd expect, expand on this by asking "Will coaching always work?" 99% of the time I would give a resounding yes, the other 1% is when human nature kicks in and either the environment or the person/persons being coached affect the progress. You can't force someone to learn and you shouldn't try.

We have to remember as well, that being the top performer doesn't mean you'll make the best coach, in fact it's very often detrimental to successful coaching.

What you need is the ability and desire to help others improve. Being able to empower people to want to be better is also a massive plus to a good coach.

In simple terms a coach should assess the current level of ability, set the outcomes for learning, agree the tactics and initiate the action to be taken and then give constructive and useful feedback so that the recipient can make sense of what's been learnt.

Having coached many people over the years I thought I'd just give you a couple of examples to show what good coaching and getting the best out of people can really do.

Let me tell you about Lori. When I first met Lori she was 17 and working part-time in her friends

Dad's newsagent (still with me?) having just given up an apprenticeship with Toni & Guy because she was fed up after spending 2 months sweeping up hair!!

I interviewed her for a telesales role and just got the feeling she'd do well with the right motivation.

Needless to say, with some support she actually did pretty well.

She went on to do very well in the recruitment industry – funny story there, she was working for a very well known recruitment company and was told by her regional sales manager that she must phone everyone on her database and sell them the new service they wanted to offer. He promptly picks a random name from the list and says.

"Here start with this guy, I'd like to hear you"

Lori looks down at the name and responds with

"I can't"

"What do you mean, you can't?"

"I mean, I cannot phone this guy and try and sell to him!"

"Why not!!" comes the angry reply.

"Well, you know all the sales skills and techniques that I have?"

"Yes!"

"Well, if I phone him and attempt to sell to him he will probably laugh"

"Why?"

"Well, that would be because he was the one who taught them to me"

"Oh"

As you may have guessed, the name was mine.

The lovely Lori has since gone on to be Sales Manager for a large building company and is doing very well for herself.

I should also mention Kirsty Jones. Who I first

met when working for a river cruise company in Gloucester and who accompanied me to deliver a presentation and training session to a call centre in Swansea.

My first piece of advice to her in preparing for the presentation etc was…

"Tell them what you're going to tell them, tell them, and then tell them what you told them."

She now quotes that same line back to me!!

She then presented to the CEO of the company she worked for and got herself a promotion by blowing away all the other candidates and also put together and delivered an excellent training course that made a big difference to the campaign the team was working on.

She's currently putting herself through a degree course to further improve herself and her career.

I bought her 'The Art of War' by Sun Tzu for her birthday, now I'm just waiting for her to start quoting it at me!!

Which brings us nicely on to...

Training…Training…Training.

As I've already mentioned, good quality, relevant training is massively important to keep people focussed and at their best – it works in the same way that coaching does, keep them up to date and motivated and things will be a lot easier.

Firstly, you can't just decide that you want to do some training because you think the team needs to improve.

For one thing a lack of training may not be your only problem!!

The best thing to do is to first conduct a Training Needs Analysis so that you can establish where the gaps in performance are and therefore deliver the right training. All sounds very simple I know but there's a couple of things you'll need to consider.

A Training Needs Analysis is used to identify the new skills, knowledge and in some instances, attitudes that your people require to meet yours and their development needs.

So, how to progress, well you'll need to identify the key priorities, any new performance goals and eliminate any obstacles that may restrict your obtaining those goals.

You should look for any gaps in peoples' competence and establish some success indicators. You should also evaluate the training at every stage.

You need to understand the areas you're going to look at in your analysis and approach each one in turn so that your analysis will give you the answers you need in order to create your training program.

Try something like this…

- ✓ The vision/mission/strategy – what end result are you aiming for.
- ✓ What performance issue are you trying to address?
- ✓ What are the specific learning objectives – what do you want them to be able to do once the training is finished

✓ An outline of the training solutions
✓ What method will you use to deliver the training
✓ Roles and responsibilities
✓ Evaluation criteria

As an example, you could try what's called a Force Field Analysis. It works like this. You write the performance goal at the top of a flip chart or something similar.

Divide the sheet into two columns and name them 'Help' and 'Hinder', then in the 'Help' column just brainstorm the things that will help people achieve the goal (the enablers) and then in the 'Hinder' column list the things that may stand in their way (the obstacles)

So if we take a simple performance goal such as 'Sell more' in the 'Help' column you would have things such as,

- High quality product
- Solid Management
- Good incentive scheme

And in the 'Hinder' column you would have

- Unclear priorities
- Lack of time
- Too much admin
- Lack of product knowledge

From this you can start to see the gaps and where you can start putting together your training program.

You'll need to map the process so you can establish the competencies. What you're aiming to do is look at where the team are now, where they need to be and lastly, how you can get them there and what training you need to deliver to achieve it.

You would do well to establish some learning objectives to accompany this and then you'll need to conduct an evaluation once training is finished.

An evaluation is usually made up of four different areas, but you may want to adapt it to suit your own needs – it's also really useful to get your delegates to fill in an evaluation sheet at the end of the program to judge the success and get some feedback.

I usually break mine down as follows;

- Reaction – did the delegates enjoy the course?
- Learning – did they learn from it?
- Behaviour – have they changed their behaviour as a result of the training?
- Results – did it have the desired result in line with your analysis?

Now you've worked out what training you feel you need to deliver, you need to look at your training and how you intend to deliver it.

Firstly, you need to consider how the people you will be training like to learn.

Adults learn differently to children. I know that sounds obvious but it's a big consideration when putting together a training course.

Adults learn basically if they need or want to.

They also learn by linking the new learning to past, present or future experience. They learn by practising what they've been taught, with help and guidance and in an informal and non-threatening environment.

Apparently, the average person thinks at roughly 400 wpm whereas they talk at about 120 wpm - unless you're me then it's probably a bit more, I do tend to get carried away sometimes!! - So, we have to account for the excess.

However interesting the content, the brain goes into auto-pilot after about 15-20 minutes if there's nothing to stimulate it!!

The trick is to be aware of this and make sure you vary your approach and what you ask the delegates to do. Get them involved, ask their thoughts and opinions, get them to do something practical. Plan regular discussion periods, group work etc.

Of course, a good trainer can use voice control to help change the pace and keep things interesting.

Remember this, if the brain is given a message once, you've got about 10% chance of it being remembered whereas if you repeat, recap and review the message it can increase to around 90%.

Add to that the whole right side/left side brain theory which states that people who use the left side of their brain are generally more logical and those that use the right side of their brain are more creative.

From a training point of view, it means that with a mixed crowd, any message or piece of information you want to get across needs to use both logical and creative in its delivery.

The best way to do this is using VHF – Visual/hearing/Feeling

Visual – pictures, images, diagrams, charts, photos

Hearing – words, music, sounds, conversations

Feeling – emotions, smells, tastes, pain/comfort.

So, you've worked out how you're going to deliver the training now you need to think about the right environment.

I appreciate that this all sounds very involved and complicated but if you get everything in place the results will speak for themselves.

Think about

- Good audio-visual equipment/flip charts etc
- Writing material/workbooks
- A good seating pattern
- Comfortable chairs
- Room temperature
- Breaks
- Lighting

The thing you must always do is plan the session, know your course timings otherwise it can get a little interesting.

Icebreakers are always good, there's hundreds out there, pick one that suits your style of delivery or if you're feeling adventurous, make up your own.

Above all, be enthusiastic in your delivery. If you're not enthusiastic about the course content why should the delegates?

Keep good eye contact, sweep your audience pausing on each person for a couple of seconds, don't turn your back on them to read from a Powerpoint presentation or your notes.

I'm sure you've all seen it before but remember Albert Mehrabians research. When we communicate the recipients understanding of the message is received in the following manner.

- 7% Words (what you say)
- 38% Tone (how you say it)
- 55% (Body Language)

There are plenty of books out there that focus entirely on this subject if you want to know more so I shan't bore you with it!

Everyone who delivers training will follow the basics but their own personality will shine through in the way they deliver. My own preferred way of delivering is very active, I very rarely, if ever sit and deliver training sessions, I am more inclined to stand and pace about the room while keeping eye contact with each delegate. I find it keeps them on their toes and focuses their attention. It's also then not much of a surprise when I ask them to do something because the delivery is so active.

If I'm honest (and I'm sure young Mr Drew will, once again, happily agree!!) I also tend to get a little excitable when I'm training because I get a tiny bit passionate about the whole thing!!

I also seem to recall him kicking me under the table at a prospective client meeting to stop me saying anything when they told me the conversions their current sales person was achieving.

"Apparently" I have my normal voice and then my excited voice or so the boys tell me – I would argue but I feel it would probably fall on deaf ears!!

I personally prefer to call it having passion for what I do but they just won't listen!

I've actually had them at sessions giggling to themselves when I change from 'normal' to 'excited'. They've even videoed me delivering training to make their point.

Chapter 4

When you arrange a callback, make sure you do it,

Even if the person isn't available to talk... professionalism breeds trust – it's just rude not to and the job is hard enough without making it harder for yourself.

What it also does, certainly in a business to business environment, is build your credibility and reliability.

What the client starts to see after a few missed callbacks, is that you do what you say you'll do, even if it's just calling when you say you will. Eventually they will give in and accept your call, then you get to do what you're paid for.

I'll throw in more tips and advice as it comes to me but those should keep you going for a bit!

Right story time, most peoples' image of a consultant is taken from the TV. Pinstripe suit, flash watch, overpaid etc, etc. These days that couldn't be further from the truth.

Now I will admit to having a couple of pinstripe suits but the watch I wear was bought for me by my son Jack at the market for Christmas, but it looks nice and he bought it for me, so I wear it.

Being a consultant, if you're any good at it, can be a roller coaster ride of meetings, Starbucks, motorways and 12 hour days…I know, sounds dead glamorous doesn't it!!

Don't get me wrong, I love every minute of it. For me it's the variety and change of scenery that I love, no two weeks the same and all that.

Just a quick piece of advice for anyone considering becoming a consultant, in any industry.

A good consultant is constantly learning both from their own efforts and from the people they work for.

For example, as you'd expect, I've delivered training on telesales many times over and I'm quite happy to say that I probably pick up a useful tit bit at the very least every time I do.

It's no good to you or your clients if you just roll out the same old thing time and again.

The call centre and telesales industry, for example, is constantly changing and updating itself so you have to move with it or get left behind...and by left behind I mean not get any work because you can't adapt.

I've helped many clients over the years ranging from the obvious call centre assignments to the more obscure.

Right, I guess the best place to start is the beginning or in the case, my first ever client.

You'll remember that the first project I undertook was for Bristol City Football Club back in the day when they weren't playing so well and season ticket sales were quite a bit down on previous years.

I was brought in by another consultant, a chap called Guy Cowper - ex-Army Tank Corp and a thoroughly decent chap - because he didn't have the telesales knowledge that I had.

I remember one meeting during that time when myself and Guy were joined by Colin Sextone one of the top dogs at the club and ex-Navy and the Commercial Manager, Richard Gould ex-Army Air Corp…talk about me being the odd one out!!

Still, it was a great first contract, down the road from my house and very well paid.

My Brothers on the other hand thought it was hilarious. Growing up I was never the biggest fan of football, so for me to be working for a football club tickled them somewhat.

It would've been very easy to get caught up in the idea that consulting was going to be easy. I look back with thanks now at the fact that my ex-wife was never particularly interested in what I do and possess a natural affliction to call centres.

When you get home from being amazing – or so you think – and you're greeted with "That's nice but we need to go shopping" it keeps you grounded and focussed, a great thing to have when you're starting out.

Next for me came a long-term project in Melksham for a marketing company working in the newspaper industry – I've already told a couple of stories from that one.

They had a 48 seat outbound call centre that wasn't quite performing how it should have been and I was called in as the Interim Operations Manager to work my magic.

Right let's get the boring stuff out of the way so we can get to the stories.

They basically phoned consumers in whichever region the local paper covered and offered them a deal on getting the paper to boost subscriptions.

When I arrived, they were pulling in approximately 500 orders a week, with a small portion of the team accounting for most of that total. Needless to say, the majority of the team needed a bit of a kick.

The MD there was an ex-Guards PT instructor named Andy Milton, who was, to say the least, a little honest with his wording!

After the first week onsite Andy and I went to lunch and amongst the discussions I remember describing his two Team Leaders as about as useful as a chocolate teapots.

The silly thing is, once he'd digested what I'd said he agreed!!

There's a saying I use quite often when first starting on projects "It's wood for the trees stuff" which is a shortened version of the old saying "You can't see the wood for the trees".

The thing is people get so caught up in running their business they can often miss the obvious things, until, with help, they stand back and take a look. So with that out of the way, we made some plans to get things firing on all cylinders again.

First thing was to inject a bit of life into the call centre.

Which basically consisted of me starting lots of games and general silliness and spending as much time as possible walking the floor.

There's a running debate as to the usefulness of 'floor walking'. Personally, I'm a big fan – partly because I've proved time and time again that it works and partly because I love doing it!!

Others find it distracting and a little excitable.

OK, back to the story. So, what happened when I started floor walking?

Well, there was an almost immediate increase in performance and a definite increase in moral. Lots of smiley happy faces, enjoying what they are doing and doing it with renewed vigour.

As I've said, everyone likes a pat on the back when they do well, whether it be physical or verbal, and when they get it every time they succeed then doing things well becomes a habit.

In a sales environment, those involved generally like there to be a constant 'buzz', an atmosphere that lifts the whole room and consequently those that are in it.

The call centre also had a need to get orders confirmed as they were made – you'll no doubt recall the earlier story and my little mishap with the numb leg etc – so being on the floor as much as possible meant I was able to not only get a great feel for how the team was feeling and performing but also to confirm orders myself and thus allowing me to check first hand what was being said on the phone.

Right, quick story, as I mentioned earlier, I once started a game of pass the parcel using pound shop crap wrapped in old newspaper.

So, here we are in a 48 seat call centre in Melksham and we need a bit of a lift. So myself and one of the girls from reception head off to town – well, I say town, we are talking about Melksham so using the word town is probably exaggerating somewhat – and raid the pound shop.

We spent £30 and bought three bags full of utter rubbish.

We get back to the office and the girls on reception start wrapping it all in the pile of old newspapers they have in the corner – you'll remember that they increase newspaper subscriptions and the clients used to regularly send them copies.

Next morning I get into my office to find a pile of pass the parcel type 'presents' ready to be deployed.

So here's the plan. When an agent gets a subscription and it's been confirmed (remember the reason for my chair issue) they ring a little bell on their desk and get to unwrap a sheet from the parcel.

I'll be honest, when I told them what we were going to do, there were several moans and groans etc but all credit to them they jumped in and gave it ago.

After 6 or 7 unwrappings it was game on.

We had grown men arguing over bags of marbles and toy soldiers.

We had sensible mothers waving around pink fluffy pens.

We also had a fantastic day of sales. It was like a bell ringing competition there were so many sales happening.

Needless to say, Andy was a happy bunny.
It just goes to show that you don't always have to spend an absolute fortune to get the desired result.

Now you know what happened when I started a game of pass the parcel.

One of the bigger issues with a larger sales team is being able to monitor them all from a performance and training point of view.

One of the more immediate areas to consider was the distinct lack of training.

You'll remember my 'chocolate teapot' comment, which kind of gave me an idea as to the approach being taken before I arrived.

The sales team obviously had targets – bronze, silver and gold as I remember – the difficulty was that for those that didn't hit the minimum target there was no consequence, they we're just stuck back on the phone next day with their fingers crossed!!

So, on day two I made a change to that, I basically announced that anyone not meeting target would spend the first hour of the next day in training with me, giving them the skills and support they would need to not only meet, but eventually beat the targets.

I know it doesn't sound like much but when you consider that they were getting no real training, support or coaching, it was a big change.

If I was to make massive and immediate changes to the whole process it would probably have had the opposite affect to what I was after.

All I did in that first hour with those under target was to get them focussed on the job at hand. I gave them some fairly generic outbound calling training and just supported them.

Again, I know it doesn't sound like much, but it was all that was needed in the initial stages and it made a great difference to the teams performance.

Obviously as time went on the content of the training intensified and those spending their first hour with me really started to move forward.

There's possibly something else I should mention at this point about my style of training...

Those that have either been trained by me or have been anyway involved in me delivering training will know exactly what I mean when I say, when I'm delivering training I struggle to stand still.

I'm not going to apologise for it, it's how I get the results that I do, but if you put me in a small room for training we may have a bit of an issue!

Let me explain – or should I say justify – why I do it the way I do. I mentioned before about the amount of time people can sensibly concentrate for so for me moving around while I'm delivering training helps me get over some of that. It also allows me to get as much eye contact as possible with delegates and keep them interested and paying attention.

It also means that the session is memorable and that the training sticks in their mind.

Don't get me wrong, it doesn't always go to plan and I have on several occasions, been caught out by my inability to remain stationary whilst in the process of delivering training.

One habit I have stopped is when involved in training/coaching, when replying to a tough question with a fabulous response, I use to say "Oh I like that, someone write that down"

It was, of course, always meant in jest but on one project having delivered several training/coaching sessions, the cheeky young ladies had, every time I said it, actually written it down and consequently presented me with a framed copy at the end of the project.

I've been given all manner of gifts etc after finishing projects and I've kept them all. I've been given my name in chocolate, wine (shame I don't drink) champagne, a very nice pen, a Swiss Army knife, several ties, cooking books, running books and a lovely framed picture of King Louie from the Jungle Book.

You remember King Louie, King of the Swingers, although the picture I was given had the 'S' crossed out therefore making him, or me to be more precise, the 'King of the Wingers'

I am reliably informed that it was created in homage to my uncanny ability to think on my feet and make things up on the spot.

Something that has saved many a situation for clients so I guess I shouldn't be too upset by the comment. All said with love I'm told.

I should, I supposed give an example…

I arrive at a clients office in Bath to deliver a day of 'Telephone Selling' training to be told by the MD that he "hadn't been able to book the room upstairs so could I deliver the training at the back of the sales room"?

"Well I could but it won't be very conducive to good working practice for everyone else because first and foremost, we're not exactly going to be sitting quietly in the corner".

My resulting fix to the situation was to pop across the road to the pub and ask to 'borrow' their function room.

I ended up delivering two sessions that day from the stage of their function room, whilst the delegates sat on the black leather sofa's usually reserved for fans of whichever band was playing that night!!

When I'm given cards or presents, for me it's a sign that I've build some good relationships, that I've done my job properly and that the client is happy with what I've done for them.

Talking of presents reminds me of a project I did for HelpHire an accident management company, at the time based in Bath - you may remember the fibre glass cable story – They were setting up a Bristol call centre of about 400 seats and I was brought in to help with the inductions.

Delivering inductions for 400 people is no mean feat, especially if you only have a small training team, hence why I was added to the mix.

The inductions were actually two weeks long and quite involved and to cope with the demand, they actually hired three what looked like old school huts and plonked them in the car park and that was where we did an awful lot of the training – not much fun in the heart of the summer!!

This is probably a good time to tell another story to show that I have, on occasion, gently pushed the boundaries…

Part of the induction at HelpHire involved walking the newbies around the two buildings to show them where everything was etc.

HelpHire lived in an old MOD set up which amounted to two, two storey buildings either end of a car park. On the ground floor of building two was the IT department and it formed the final part of the tour before we headed back to the training room.

So, I walk into the department with 15 newbies in tow and politely announce "This is the IT department, where they open and close windows"

Now we all know that the standard answer for all people in IT when you say your computer's not working is either "Turn it on and then off again" or something along the lines of "Have you closed ….. down and restarted it" but apparently stating that fact is not a popular choice!!

It took the length of the car park for them to

phone over and have a moan. In my defence, what they didn't hear me say afterwards was "All joking aside, the guys are great and always happy to help" but there you go.

Liability day was always a bit of a giggle. The aim of the day was for the newbies to get an understanding of liability, who was responsible etc. The way this was done was with a box of toy cars and one of those kids rugs that depicts a town with roads etc. Great fun was had by all setting up accidents and then debating who was at fault.

Although this was also the project where I was asked to write a telephone selling training session, but I wasn't allowed to call it sales!!

It was this that prompted a rather interesting meeting a week or so later. I'm sat around a table with the usual crowd of people and the discussion turns to the training session.

I argued that not calling it a sales course was a little pointless as the content was obviously going to be sales focussed. This was met with the response from one of the Team Leaders,

"But we're not a sales company"

"I beg to differ" I replied

"No, we're definitely not a sales company, we don't do sales"

This is where I start to get a bit naughty…

"So what you're telling me is that every person that we phone or that phones us, takes the service?"

"No of course not!"

"OK, so what stops them?"

"Well, generally it's the collision damage waiver" came the confident reply.

"So if someone says no to the service, what do we do?"

"Well, we tell them about the benefits of having it and how it would be better for them"

Out of the corner of my eye I can see the

Operations Director slowly lowering his head to his hands and he watches me casually walk the poor Team Leader into the hole she's digging for herself.

"So what you're telling me is that if we speak to someone who doesn't really want the service, we try and persuade them to have it by offering them some benefits?"

"Exactly!"

"OK, but isn't that sales?"

Oddly enough, it was a little silent after that.

For me it's always a little odd that people in business try as hard as they can not to be a 'sales' company, but if you think about it, there isn't a single company that can survive without sales. It may be a bit more prominent and obvious with some businesses but everyone has to make a sale for their business to work.

That being said and to get back on track with talking about the HelpHire project, it's worth noting that the Bristol centre was outperforming the existing operation in Bath within 6 months and then merged back into Bath to reduce costs and to be able to better share the Bristol best practice that we'd helped to create.

I did manage to gain a couple of great friends out of it so it wasn't all bad. I also apparently gained the nick name 'Trouble' although I can't for the life of me think why…

Now as I've said, over the years, I've completed projects for many different clients in lots of different industries.

One of the most obscure was a project for a veterinary practice.

I have to say that if you'd asked me at the beginning of my career to name the type of business that I'd be working with, I'm convinced that vets would not have been on that list.

Nevertheless and not being one to shy away from a challenge, I accepted the project and got straight to it.

The idea was to set up a team to phone their 25,000+ database and offer them free delivery on cat/dog food.

One of the funniest things that happened during this project was actually nothing to do with telephones. As you'd expect the deliveries were made by van and on this occasion, the van driver had phoned in sick and nobody was free to take his place. So not wanting to have the whole process grind to a halt by such a simple problem, I say.

"I'll do it"

Now driving a van around Bristol to deliver some pet food may not sound overly taxing, but this was the winter a few years ago when we had thick snow on the ground.

Let's look at that picture again shall we, there I am in my suit, humping pet food up and down driveways in Clifton (for those that don't know, it's a fairly posh part of Bristol) in the snow.

There were several times that day that I gently pressed the brakes on the van and then crossed my fingers and prayed that the van wouldn't hit anything it shouldn't whilst happily sliding through the snow and ice.

I never really understood how much money people spend on their pets until I did that project.

I've already told a story or two about the call centre in Melksham so it's probably time for a bit more.

The MD at the call centre was very motivation focussed so let me pretty much have free reign on what I did to keep the team excited (I'm sure there are a couple of people reading this who are now wondering how mad he was to do that but we had fun so that's all that matters!!)

During the several months I was there we had all manner of activities, such as Space Hopper races up and down the call centre, pin the tail on the donkey, egg and spoon races we even started games of basketball and so on in the car park.

The guys there would take any opportunity to dress up so Halloween etc were always welcomed with open arms.

Motivation was played a huge part in that call centre and we were continually thinking of new ways to keep it going.

You'll remember the Pass the Parcel story

Lucky dip with an old fish tank and some sawdust also worked fairly well.

As I've already mentioned I'm a big fan of floor walking and Melksham was excellent proof that it works. When you've got 48 people on the phone spread across the whole floor then you can't just sit at your desk and hope to keep track of everything. I know someone will pipe up with the argument about technology doing it for you etc but for me there is no replacement for being on the floor with your team, keeping them motivated and performing at their best, especially in a call centre environment.

Just to balance things out and put the good with the bad, one of the downsides to the Melksham call centre was its position. At one end of the car park was the office and at the other end was a petrol station.

Very convenient I hear you say.

Unfortunately, yes it was, all too convenient for buying crisps and chocolates!

Although I do remember starting a game of British Bulldogs in the aforementioned car park, along with an impromptu game of basketball – we had no nets so I had to get two of the lads to stand with their arms in a circle in front of them...

What it boils down to for me has always been that you cannot leave them to their own devices and expect it to work – especially when you're dealing with a sales team.

It never ceases to amaze me that the first person to moan or be surprised is the one that left them alone with no support or back up and then is surprised when they fail or miss target.

Call centres and telesales operations have moved on in leaps and bounds over the last few years – I remember having the data I had to call handed to me as a printed spreadsheet – but I still say that there is absolutely no substitute for standing alongside your team or teams and showing them that you are behind them – a congratulatory pat on the back can work just as well as a physical prize.

Chapter 5

Now seems like a good time to tell you about some of the other clients I've worked with and the stories that go with them.

Let's talk about 5* serviced apartments and a New Zealander named Andrew Brown.

Andy asked me to come and give his sales team a bit of a boost in preparation for the arrival of a new Sales Manager.

Consequently, I put together a five week plan to do just that which involved delivering some training and then coaching.

This was the first time I'd been asked by a client to evaluate employees suitability for a role and it felt a little odd to have my professional opinion result in two people losing their jobs.

I regret to say that it was not the last time I was asked to do this and you never get used to it, you do however, do what you can to make it painless for all affected and whenever possible I try and offer as much help and support as I can to anyone involved.

I do recall another story from working with those guys. The area they had their office is one of Bristols' more salubrious areas and I used to park my car in one of the surrounding side streets.

No drama I hear you say, let me explain…

On the morning in question, I'd got into town a bit earlier than normal so was sat in my car, in a suit, making a couple of phone calls.

To say that a bloke sat in car, in a suit, stood out like a sore thumb would be an understatement.

Two minutes later, a rather large gentleman knocks on my window and asks what I'm waiting for.

"Just waiting to go to work" I say and he walks away nodding.

For those that know Bristol, I was sat in a family

saloon, wearing a suit in the middle of St. Pauls.

Now, having served as a doorman in Bristol's pubs and clubs in my younger days, I'm perfectly able to stand up for myself...I'm also smart enough to know when to shut up and pick my battles!!

It just goes to show that when you're starting out it's not all champagne and caviare...come to think of it, it still isn't...

Over the years I've worked with lots of clients and some of them have had offices in some obscure and interesting places.

For example, I did a training/coaching project for Stephens & George, a huge print company in Merthyr Tydfil (which I swear means 'Middle of nowhere' in English!) and on my way to go and see them, as I got closer to their building my Sat Nav just stopped working – now I don't mean the battery went flat or anything like that, I mean it just stopped working, like we'd entered the twilight zone!!

Thankfully, their building is that big, everyone knows where it is.

Let me give you an idea of how big it is. I walked with the MD's wife, the length of the factory from reception to the training rooms when I arrived, but because we were chatting I didn't really pay much attention to the route.

So, at the end of the day, I say to the delegates,

"One of you had better show me the way out or I might still be here tomorrow"

"I'll take you" says young Courtney

With that we walk out of the building, get in his car and drive to reception. Yes you heard me correctly, we drove to reception because it was quicker!

I also drove down to Hampshire to deliver some training etc for Nick Findlay at Premiere Business Audio.

Now on this occasion I had Steve Drew with me and we happily followed the directions from the Sat Nav until we ended up in a field with nothing to see except trees and grass expecting to hear duelling banjos any second!

In his defence, Nick did tell us that the offices were a bit 'out of the way' but this was taking that a bit far.

After a quick call and a bit of manoeuvring we arrived at the office and I can safely say that it is the first time I'd seen a gaggle of geese walk past the window in the middle of a meeting!

The project itself was an interesting one. The Team Leader was in all fairness, at the time, quite inexperienced and the team were, to say the least, taking advantage of that fact.

To her credit she took in everything we went through and has now moved up in her career.

We did some personality profiling, designed some training and then after we'd delivered it, helped her set up a solid coaching process.

Some of it was really simple tweaks and changes, for example, marking the teams target down each time they got an appointment (sale) rather than it going upwards.

Psychologically that's much better because eventually the target disappears down to zero when they've hit it.

Bramble Crest was another 'middle of nowhere' office. It's basically an old aircraft hanger out near Cirencester.

As I'm sure you're starting to learn, there's a funny story attached to this project…

I'm in the office, chatting through the plan with Chris the FD, she takes a phone call and being polite (and needing the loo) I say,

"That's OK, you take that, and I'll pop to the toilet"

"OK, great, Carol will show you where they are"

I step out of the office and ask Carol where I need to go.

Her first action is to hand me a high viz jacket – a bright pink one I hasten to add – and then points me to the door. I have to walk through the warehouse, out of the back door and around the corner to the toilet block. I should explain that the aforementioned aircraft hanger is on an old RAF base.

Any other time I went to see them, I learnt my lesson, I drive round the corner and go to the loo first!

We did lots of training with the folks at Bramble Crest, they're not what you'd call a standard call centre so we had to go through a range of stuff such as communication skills, complaint handling, time management and so on.

They sit in an almost retail environment as they supply garden furniture so lots of customer contact.

One really fun project we did was for The Holiday Lodge Group. As you may have guessed from the name, they are involved in the holiday lodge industry, which I knew very little about until they asked me to get involved and help them set up an internal sales team.

These guys were based in Bradford-on-Avon, which for those that have never been there is very much a stereo-typical English village kind of place with a river running through the middle. Because we were setting up from scratch we had to do everything from start to finish, so we were deep in the throws of recruiting sales staff while ordering desks, phones etc.

When we had the team recruited and everything was in place we put together some training and were basically ready for the off – I was also staying on a bit longer to settle the team down and deal with any teething problems.

We put a couple of weeks behind us and then the whole company charged off to attend the Caravan & Camping Show at Newbury Showground because we all agreed it would be a great way for all of us to have a look at the industry, some of the prominent players etc.

Now the name Newbury Showground sounds very grand – don't you believe it, the 'Showground' is actually just a big field off the M4!!

The guys actually took a stand at the show so that we could get involved, give out some flyers, chat to prospective customers etc and it was then that I had my first view of a 'proper' holiday lodge.

The place was better than the house I lived in at the time and had a hot tub on the roof!!

Some of those lodges are really impressive. On another occasion we drove down to the South coast to take a look at the lodges the company owned – again, really nice and what a view.

Now just to show that I'm not adverse to working on a Saturday rather than send someone else to do it, I remember a trip to Melksham with Stewart Kemble to deliver some customer service/communication skills sessions at Valldata.

It's also worth mentioning that in my travels up and down the country, I've come across some absolutely fantastic operations and I've also come across some not so fantastic operations.

One of the nicest I've had the pleasure of attending was the offices of Nominet near Oxford.

Very nice offices, very advisor focussed and an entirely pleasant place to go to to deliver training.

I've actually been there a couple of times in support of Demitris Edwards from Vocall to deliver customer service and communication skills training. It's one of those places that trainers generally love going to because not only is it a supportive and well equipped environment, the advisor population actually welcome the opportunity to learn – which as a trainer makes life so much easier!

Nominet was also the first place that I saw changeable desks in use – the ones that convert upwards so that people can stand while they work without having to slouch over.

Very cool idea and something I wish I'd had when I was working the phones!

And in the interest of fair play, I'll tell you about one of the more 'interesting' places I attended.

All I'll say is that it was in Bristol and I was sat in this guys' office discussing how he wanted to set up a 'funky' call centre to book appointments for his field team.

My first and most obvious questions was,

"OK, do you have a space in mind?"

"You're sitting in it" comes the reply.

So, I turn around in my chair to survey the room behind me and its 'funkiness'

I kid you not, around three sides of the room is fitted with what I can only describe as a rather gaudy patterned kitchen work top about two foot deep and then placed at regular intervals are a bunch of breakfast bar stools.

I turned back round expecting to see the team from 'Punked' but instead see the guy sat there staring at me grinning like a Cheshire cat, like he's found the golden ticket!

As those that know me well enough will no doubt confirm, I'm rarely lost for words but on this occasion all that I could eventually manage was to utter "Are you kidding?"

I can just see the HR professionals reading this counting the number of issues this would cause them!

Needless to say I didn't take that project!

To keep this train of thought, there's been some interesting conversations over the years and some interesting locations.

I remember doing a project for a company called Ecovision who's offices were actually based on the edge of Highgrove estate. I can assure you it's a little unnerving to have armed police walk past the office!!

I also remember a long time friend of mine, Natalie Rosato coming to visit the office in a professional capacity. Now the office had steps and a loose gravel car park. Looked very nice but didn't mix well with Natalie's high heels and she narrowly avoided face planting the ground in full view of everyone – but I seem to remember promising that I wouldn't tell that story…

It's also a great ego boost when someone who has had fantastic success, is recognised as an expert in their industry and who's books you've read, phones you for advice.

I met Jonathon Jay a few years ago and when he

wanted to set up a calling team for his latest venture, he called me to come and help make sure it got a good start.

I've also had a lot of people send me in to their clients on their behalf.

For example, Hugo Jacobs from Lumley Jacobs sent me in to a couple of their insurance clients.

The first one was Towergate in Cheltenham.

We were delivering a training and coaching session based around one of Lumley Jacobs products.

It was in the middle of the summer and we were in one of the training rooms – a training room that had no air conditioning and windows that only opened a couple of inches.

As I've mentioned, I tend to wander around when I'm delivering sessions but on this occasion I spent most of the time stood with my back to the barely open window trying not to collapse through heat exhaustion!!

It was a little on the warm side and I made sure that I added in far more audience participation than I would normally do just so they didn't doze off from the heat.

Carol Nash up near Manchester was another one I did for Hugo. That was a two day training and coaching project that involved the usual overnight stay.

I've lost count of the amount of hotels I've stayed in over the years and no matter how many times I've done it, I still don't like going down to the restaurant and eating on my own.

It was at Carol Nash during a break in training, that I got collared by one of the other trainers with a slightly confused look on her face.

"Is everything OK?"

"Absolutely, why do you ask?" I reply

"Well, I've just never heard so much laughter coming from a training room before"

After I'd had a little giggle to myself I replied

"Don't know if I should say sorry or thank you"

Not the first time I've heard a remark like that and hopefully not the last. I've said it before, training etc has to be memorable and has to sink in, personally I use a lot of stories to get my point across, surprising I know. The theory being they may not remember the 'technical' content of the topic - especially if there's a lot of content to get through – but they generally remember the story and that tends to jog their memory for the 'technical' stuff.

For example, when I'm delivering sales training I very often tell the fridge buying story, which everyone remembers and perfectly makes my point. It's used to show the difference between people buying with logic or emotion.

It goes like this, when people are deciding what to buy they are generally thinking 'What's in it for me?'.

So off we go on a lovely Saturday morning to buy a fridge/freezer (you can imagine my excitement) after visiting several stores and losing my will to live we finally stand in front of two models that are identical in almost every way, same size, capacity, energy rating etc the only difference is that one of them is white and one is grey (and the grey one is £50 more expensive).

I ask you, which one do you think we bought?

That's right, the grey one, and do you know why?

Because it will match the handles on the kitchen doors…

It's a simple story but it makes the point and people remember it.

People buy on emotion, not logic.

Why should we train and develop our staff?

It's a question that I get asked on a regular basis and one that sometimes takes a lot of persuading.

Over the years I've designed and delivered many, many training programs and sessions to thousands of people and one of the biggest concerns once it's all over is "Will it be worth it".

Obviously I'm going to say yes, otherwise I'm going to look a bit silly, but the fact remains that good quality, relevant and sustainable training will pay for itself very quickly (It's the main reason I don't ever deliver 'off the shelf' sessions because each client is different and you have to make it fit want they want, not want you want.)

That being said, let's look at it for a moment. You employ someone with a view to them doing a job for you, so if you don't give them the tools they need to do that job, how can you possibly criticise them when they falter?

Training and developing your team means that they can do the job you pay them for.

What you'll also find is that if you give your team regular, consistent training not only will they do the job you're paying them for, but they're more likely to enjoy it and stay for the long term – a huge benefit for your business.

I have no desire to repeat myself, but this is worth saying again. Keeping your team well trained and up to date will ensure that they not only have the tools to do it, but that they enjoy doing it and as a result, your customers will reap the rewards (as will your bottom line)

It's always really satisfying when we put together a new training/coaching program for a client to get them on the right road and they start to see the benefits, along with the happy smiling faces of their team.

Just think about what you want them and the business to do/achieve and then find someone who can implement it for you

All this begs the question, how much support is enough?

I've personally mentored a few people in my career and it's very satisfying to see them succeed knowing that you've had a hand in their development etc.

For pure clarification, Mentoring is a process by which a more skilled or experienced person, serves as a role model and assists a less experienced person in their professional development.

There are lots of situations where mentoring is very useful, in the contact centre industry the most common use of it is to assist a new employee in the transition from induction to live calls.

The relationship between mentor and mentee is massively important and can actually make or break the success of the person being mentored. It's also a very fine line between just telling them what to do and actually mentoring them – by this I mean taking the time to encourage and develop the other person.

I've always seen the benefit of having a mentor or just someone to bounce ideas off and I still do it now, it's great to be stuck in the "can't see the wood for the trees" situation and then have someone with a fresh viewpoint give you some clarity – or in what has often been the case for me, Paul Anslow telling me that "I'm doing it again"

There are no hard and fast rules for who should be a mentor, although certainly in the call centre environment it tends to be senior agents or Team Leaders that initially take on that role.

There's often a comparison between mentoring and coaching and in fact training and there's no real exact definition, as it can rely quite heavily on opinion.

But in theory, coaching tends to have a more specific focus on a certain skill, training tends to be work related and concentrates on specific tasks whereas mentoring is more about support and advice and can on occasion encompass all three.

Mentoring is about helping someone to understand what is expected of them and then helping them to meet that expectation.

Having been a mentor and a mentee the following definition has worked well for me over the years.

Mentors

- Don't expect to have all the answers
- Avoid being judgmental
- Be clear about expectations and boundaries
- Maintain regular contact
- Respect the confidentiality

Mentee

- Accept the challenge
- Be active in your own development
- Build the relationship/trust with your mentor
- Have open discussions
- Don't expect everything to happen overnight

Keeping things on track

Anyone in the industry knows that successfully operating a call centre or telesales operation can be a constant struggle against hitting the KPIs and keeping the staff happy and motivated.

Knowing where to get started, whilst keeping all the plates spinning is a challenge in itself and the bigger the operation, generally the bigger the headache!

So what can you do about it...

Chapter 6

Over the years we've come to realise that there was a need to simplify the process of looking at the overall performance of an operation. With that in mind we set about creating a methodology that would allow us to take a holistic view of all the elements involved in creating that desired success.

The result is what we call the Performance Improvement Matrix (PIM) and it's the process we've used successfully with clients.

It works like this, the Performance Improvement Matrix (PIM) takes centre stage in a brain storming session where each aspect is looked at in turn and desired actions are agreed, thus creating a 'plan of action'.

We've actually found that using a huge white board or sheet of paper for the brain storming session gets the best results.

Since its inception it has proved invaluable in terms of the ability to regularly assess the performance of their operation and make those necessary 'tweaks' to continue improving.

The basic premise is that all parts of the matrix are integral to running a successful call centre or telesales operation and getting them to work together in unison reduces the headaches and makes for a much smoother operation.

Now you won't necessarily have to make changes or adjustments to all parts of the matrix, but it's certainly worth while making sure. The overall aim is to get all parts working together and not to the detriment of each other.

A 'Review Document' is a good starting point – basically a couple of pages of standard questions that gives us a basic outline of where you are at the moment and helps to focus on the job at hand.

Look at it this way, what you're looking at is a simple process map. You're at A and you want to be at B, so what do you need to change, adjust, put in place to get there. Therefore establishing where you are at the current time is a sensible place to start.

You can put together your own list of questions (or ask us and we'll do it for you) but to give you a start point you probably need to ask things like,

1. Current team structure (and is it working?)
2. What ongoing training is provided?
3. What ongoing coaching is provided?
4. Calling hours?
5. Current KPIs (and are they being met)?
6. Facilities in place?
7. Environment?

Now, the thing to understand is that all parts are connected, for example, having call recording in place means that calls can be used as a training tool, which means that you can improve performance. The right CRM system will allow for effective reporting, therefore making setting the right targets/KPI's much easier. I'm sure you get the picture...

What you need to do next is take your review document answers and match it up to the Performance Improvement Matrix (PIM).

Which looks like this;

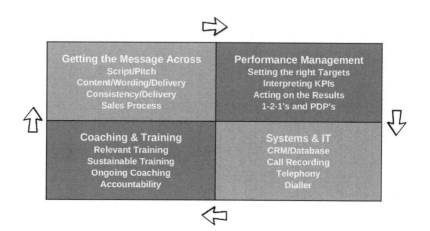

We'll go through each square separately so that
you can in turn break down each aspect of your
operation and make sure you're ticking all the
boxes.

Hopefully we'll find out that you've got
everything nailed and you're well on your way to
the efficient running operation that you are aiming
for.

If not, then at least we'll find out which area
needs some attention and what you need to do to
get it back on track.

OK, let's take a look at each piece of the puzzle…

Getting the message across.

Once you've done your review document you should have something to revert back to when going through the process and the first thing to look at is whether or not the message is getting across to customers properly.

By this I mean, do your agents give a performance when delivering their pitch or do they just go through a question and answer session?

You have to remember that most customers, whether B2B or B2C will be receiving several phone calls a week (or sometimes a day!) so you have to ensure that your call stands out.

The way to do this is to make sure that firstly the content and wording of the 'script' (if you choose to use one) is relevant and interesting – I always try and adapt the Attention, Interest, Desire, Action (AIDA) approach as my basic start point, it's a bit old school but it works perfectly well.

You have to make sure that not only is it delivered in such a way that it engages your customer but also that it is delivered in the same manner consistently. Once you've got a delivery that you're happy with, you need to make sure that the sales process is consistent with it and that it works.

You also need to ensure that the process works for the customer – just because it works for you, it doesn't necessarily stand that it will create a good customer journey, so it pays to consider both sides. Customers are much more in tune with what they want these days and it's not always about the money!

A disjointed delivery coupled with an erratic sales process only serves to play up to the image that most people have of the call centre/telesales industry but it also makes life much more difficult than it needs to be.

The same principal does, of course, apply in terms of customer service calls. The message has to be clear and consistent, but above all it has to be customer centric.

You should regularly assess the effectiveness of the pitch your team are delivering, is it getting the result/response you want? Do the team actually follow it? Does it cover everything the customer needs to know? And so on.

Coaching & Training

Both are vital to the smooth and effective running of your operation and its longevity.

The training you deliver to your agents needs to be relevant to the job you are asking them to do. You cannot expect to roll out the same old thing and expect it to work. Times change and so should you.

The training you give them must be sustainable, by this I mean it has to be delivered in such a way that they take it in and remember it. If they don't then you'll just be showing them the same thing every three months and not really gaining any momentum.

The part where people often come unstuck is that they don't keep the coaching going. When it comes to coaching being successful, you have to make it part of your ongoing strategy. All those involved have to understand the importance of coaching their teams on a regular basis. For front line staff that should be every week. I would personally recommend twice each week.

For example, conduct a coaching session Monday or Tuesday and then a second session a couple of days later.

This works well because, in the first session you can pick up on any hurdles from the previous week and plan any changes and then in the second session you are able to either ensure that the behaviours suggested in the first session were actioned or you can re-iterate them.

Which brings me nicely on to accountability. If there is no accountability across your operation (from top to bottom) then it becomes very hard to firstly, make any kind of forward plan and secondly, no accountability means no responsibility which basically leads to your operation floundering and therefore not performing.

Performance Management

This may sound somewhat obvious, but if you don't manage the performance of your team or teams properly then they are unlikely to perform at the level you require.

First and foremost, you have to set the right targets.

Again, an obvious statement, but unfortunately, one that is overlooked all too often. You have to set targets that benefit the business but also that are obtainable. I'm sure you've all heard of

S.M.A.R.T.

• Specific
• Measurable
• Achievable
• Realistic
• Time sensitive

It's a process that's been around for quite some time, the reason being is that it works.

The targets you set have to work for everyone. They have to meet the needs of the business but they also have to not seem unobtainable to the staff having to hit them. If the targets seem completely out of reach to the team they are likely to have the reverse affect and they won't bother trying to hit them.

Once you've established the targets you'll need to record the performance so that you can see whether or not you're getting close.
That's where the KPIs (Key Performance Indicators) come in.

All too often I've seen KPIs ignored and yet they can tell you so much about how your team is performing.

Knowing how to interpret the results shown on any reports you may get, is a skill that should be paramount for any manager. You should establish first and foremost, what the ideal result looks like – whether that's in terms of sales, response times, calls handled etc – and then be able to compare the results you actually get with that 'benchmark'.

Performance Management Setting the right targets Interpreting KPIs acting on the results 1-2-1's and PDP

Reading the reports and saying to yourself "That's not good enough" will not change it, you have to be prepared to act on what you see. I know that sounds obvious, but you'd be surprised and how many times I've seen them ignored.

Let's take a sales team report as an example.

You have an agent who's making lots of calls but isn't getting any sales – it could be that they're new and struggling to handle objections, that's a training/coaching issue coupled with a concern over the data it's costing you.

You could have an agent that gets lots of sales but has a high cancellation rate – it could be that they are cutting corners in what they tell customers just to get the sale, that's a behavioural conversation and not great for your reputation.

As you can see, being able to pull out of the reports what's actually happening can dictate your next actions.

Which brings us nicely to 1-2-1's and PDP's.

1-2-1's need to happen on a regular basis and not just on the back of something you've noticed in a report. In fact, if you conduct regular 1-2-1's then you may be able to avoid some of the 'hiccups' that come from not paying enough attention to your team.

PDP's are normally a follow on from 1-2-1's and take the form of the route the agent wants to take in terms of the role within the business. It should include an action plan agreed by you and the agent in terms of their performance, behaviour, attitude etc. It's about you helping them grow as an employee and a valued member of the team. Try not to dictate to them what you expect, it's better to utilise the coaching skills you use to get from them what it is they're looking for and (from your viewpoint) how that fits with the goals of the business.

It's always useful to use the SMART process when completing a PDP with someone, that way both sides have agreed and know what is expected.

Systems & IT

It's all too easy to rely too much on the systems and IT and it's also very easy to ignore them. I would suggest that you take either route at your peril.

The first thing to look at is your CRM and database. If your database isn't clean and up to date, then it will make a mess of your CRM.

Think about how you collect your data, is it given freely by customers or is it collated through your marketing efforts?

Following that, think about whether or not your CRM is fit for purpose?

Does it allow your team to do and find everything they need/want?

Is it user friendly? I've seen some wonderfully complicated CRM's over the years, they look great but don't really help much! I've also seen some very simple ones that are perfectly good for what you need. Don't get caught up in the bells and whistles, work out what you want it to do for you and then find a system that does it.

The moral of this little story is to make sure the CRM you use is fit for purpose (your purpose, not anyone else's) and keep your database up to date and clean. Do both of these and life will be much easier.

Call recording has always been the subject of discussion in the industry, again I've come across many of them over the years and many reasons for implementing them.

In simple terms there are, I guess, two main reasons for having calls recorded.

1. From a compliance point of view and to therefore keep you and your customers safe.
2. From a training point of view.

Systems & IT CRM/Database Call recording Telephony Dialler

Both of course have their place and are equally beneficial, in fact in many instances the two go hand in hand. What you have to do is decide which reason you have for recording calls and how involved you'd like the system to be.

If you feel it necessary then you can get some all singing, all dancing systems that will allow you to not only record calls but also to listen to them as they happen and therefore train your team as it happens – whisper mode is great, although I would advise letting the agents know because it's a little off putting to be in the middle of a call and suddenly have your manager talking in your ear!!

It's also worth asking agents to select 'their best call' each week and listen to it together – these are great for playing back at team meetings (with the agents' permission obviously) as a training tool.

Compliance is a whole different ball game, if that's why you need to record calls then your biggest concern is going to be the clarity of the recording – don't forget that if you're taking card payments etc that you need to be PCI compliant. The telephony that you install and use is always going to be important and much like with everything else, it has to be fit for purpose. As with everything in this section, decide what you want it to do and then find a system that delivers it. You also need to make sure that they system you choose is compatible with a decent headset.

The phone and headset that the agents use is vital in providing a clear delivery (and service) to your customers and for them to do the job you're asking them to do properly.

If you have a large amount of data to call, then it

may well be worth using a dialler but as with anything else be careful not to get caught up in a lovely brochure or great sales pitch. Diallers have their place, but then so does click to dial from a spreadsheet. You have to decide whether or not it's an expense that you need or whether you're doing it to improve performance/efficiency.

I've had the conversation many times with clients about this topic and very often they are buying into the idea of a dialler because your team aren't calling enough is very possibly a false economy – look at your team and the training/coaching you're giving them, it may well be that you can save yourself the expense of a dialler just by getting behind them more.

If you consider everything in the Performance Improvement Matrix then you won't go far wrong, we've been personally using it for clients and our own call centres for quite a while.

Regular training and coaching is massively important. Be consistent in everything you do and use the reports for your benefit, they'll help you huge amounts in knowing what's going on and what you need to do about it.

The bottom line with most of this stuff is to make sure you have the right reason for doing it and that with equipment or hardware that it's fit for purpose.

You can of course add recruitment into the mix, but that's a whole different ball game and one that

I generally leave to the experts.

On the subject of getting experts to do things for you, let's just take a moment to talk about recruitment.

There are lots of things in our industry that can be classed as a 'necessary evil' and for me it's recruitment.

Before I go on, I'm just going to straight away say thank you to those lovely people in recruitment who have taken away the burden for me. These lovely ladies, have carried me through many a recruitment process and curbed my frustrations to say the least.

In fact poor Natalie (you'll remember the high heels and gravel car park story) had to spend two days in a hotel in the middle of nowhere helping me deliver (and when I say deliver, I mean not kill anyone!) assessment days, I even dragged her into giving an impromptu presentation to show the delegates what we wanted – it's why I never forget her birthday!

It's always amazed me that pretty much every CV that has ever come across my desk has stated that the writer is "Excellent working on their own and working in a team". Much to the above mentioned ladies dismay I have taken to making people in interviews actually pick one of the two. I don't particularly mind which one they pick, I just want them to make a decision.

Handshakes are another thing, so many people don't seem to realise that the strength (or not) of your handshake is going to give an impression of you, rightly or wrongly, to the person interviewing you etc.

And what about dress code for interviews. It's really easy to understand folks, if you're going to see someone and expect them to give you a job then make some effort. My theory is this, if in your approach to coming to ask me for a job you can't even be bothered to make an effort with your appearance, then I'm naturally going to assume that this will be your attitude to your work, which I'm not going to want in my business.

Now I will happily agree that for some people, interviews are a bit on the scary side and as an interviewer you need to make allowances for this and having been involved in thousands of them over the years I've seen some fantastic ones and I've seen some absolutely horrendous ones. I guess the moral of the story is just prepare. Dress for the occasion, know who you're talking to and do some research. Give a good handshake and don't try and give the answer you think they want to hear.

I may talk more about recruitment later but it brings me to tears, so I may just do what I always do and pass the buck to Natalie.

It is after all only a small part of what we get involved in and when you think about who your clients are (or are going to be) you need to be clear and offer a solution.

I appreciated that that sounds very obvious, but so

many businesses (including myself when I first started) fall into the trap of not doing it, purely because they are under the misconception that because they know what they do, that it will be obvious to any prospective client. Not so I'm afraid…

I've mentioned this before I know, but it still makes me giggle. It took my dear Mother about three years to work out what her little boy does for a living and in doing so coined the phrase "If you want a call centre, he can build it for you but if you've already got one that isn't working, he'll fix it for you" and always said with a huge grin on her face, like she'd solved one of the worlds' great mysteries.

I should add that she could also perfectly explain the off-side rule!

It's been refined somewhat since then, hopefully it's all very clear to everyone now, so let me put my money where my mouth is and test the theory.

This is (briefly) how we defined it…

Customer Service Teams - Empower your people to become true front line ambassadors - Your customer service team need to deliver outstanding service on each and every call - we give them the knowledge, skills and enthusiasm to embody your brand to the greatest effect.

Sales Teams - Enhanced skills, behaviours and performance of your sales teams - direct sales can be one of the most effective and cost efficient methods of gaining new business - we teach your team the essential skills for building positive and long term relationships and getting those all important sales.

Leaders - Develop your Team Leaders & Managers to become the driving force of your success - the very best leaders engage and inspire their teams and we show them the techniques and ideas to enable them to do so.

Trainers & Coaches - Build on existing effectiveness to guarantee long term success and ROI - ongoing training and coaching is vital for long term success and we will help you develop and embed a strategy that is sustainable and effective.

That's it in a nut shell (and I'm hoping it made sense!). Clients generally came to us not necessarily because something's wrong, but because they want to be better. And because we're clear about what we do and offer a solution to their problem, everyone understands what's expected etc.

The moral of the story?

Know what it is you can do for people and the problem it solves for them - it's not about how great you are, it's about fixing a problem they have and therefore making things easier for them - don't try and be all things to all men, it doesn't work.

Know who your ideal customer is and focus on them.

OK, back to normality.

I've done a huge amount of training and coaching over the years based around the voice and what you can or cannot do with it.

Can you change your voice?

If you work in the call centre and telesales environment, some would say that your voice is quite possibly your most important tool.

To a certain extent, I would agree. It's not the be all and end all but it's certainly hugely important to get it right...and we've all heard the opposite of that I'm sure.

When you consider that what we do is possibly communication at its finest, the way you use your voice can make or break a call.

Imagine trying to sell something but you're not very clear and mumble through your pitch?

Not very likely to get the result you want.

Or the other side of the coin, imagine the result of a customer service call if the recipient thinks the tone of your voice means you're not interested...

We could, I'm sure, go on all day with comparisons and horror stories!

Just to clarify, I'm not suggesting that you try and physically change your voice when you're on the phone, that just not sensible or sustainable. What I'm saying is that being more aware of how you can use your voice is a skill and will have an effect on how successful you are.

We always put training for this type of thing into our sessions but as we feel it's getting more and more important and with the rise of social media and it being more prominent it's becoming even more important to understand your voice and how it can work for you.

As I've mentioned before, it's started some very lively debates over the years.

Among other things, it looks at things like pitch, pace, tone and what difference they make.

Why what you say and how you say it has an effect on customers.

How to be more aware of your voice, how it sounds and what you can do to get better results for the calls you deliver.

Now in a sales environment it can be even more prevalent, so how much support or leeway to you give them?

We've all no doubt heard phrases such as "The sales team are a law unto themselves" and such like but how does that happen, I'm sure businesses don't set out to create such teams...or do they?

Letting your sales team 'run away with itself' is a very easy mistake to make and if you're not careful can happen without you knowing.

Several times over the years I have been engaged by clients to 'straighten out' their sales team and the first question I ask is why they think it needs straightening out.

There are any number of answers to that questions and I shan't bore you with all of them. What I will say is that it normally happens when a business is growing and gets more concerned with revenue rather than any kind of process or best practice.

Now don't get me wrong, I completely understand that, when you're trying to build a business, as one of my old bosses used to say 'cash is king'. You can have the greatest business ever started, but without revenue it's nothing. But what tends to happen is that the sales team are allowed to 'get away with things' because they have brought in revenue and the more revenue they bring in the more they are allowed to get away with and so the vicious circle begins.

The difficulty arises when the business realises that the sales team maybe be just a little out of hand and decides to bring them back in line.

What follows is what can only be described as 'backlash' to cries of "but we've always been allowed to do it" etc.

What generally needs to happen is to revert to basics, put in place (and enforce) some standard behaviours and practices and to, of course, show the team how it will benefit them and help them to actually make more sales.

It's not an easy project to undertake and you have to be prepared for some 'tension' whilst you're doing it but it can be done and it does make a difference.

My advice to avoid having to go through this is to make sure that you have everything in place whilst you build your team, get it right and then it's just a case of escalation. If you build on something solid you're less likely to have any drama – although we are talking about sales teams and a bit of drama tends to 'come with the territory! Break it down into specific areas and work on each part with the team – if they help you build it the foundation will be much stronger.

This reminds me of a client where this was the exact problem they were facing. By their own admission they had grown fantastically well but in doing so they had let things fall by the wayside and now realised that if they didn't get to grips with it pretty soon then all hell was likely to break loose.

What they had was a team of sales people of varying ages and personalities that had got into the habit of doing what they wanted, when they wanted to do it. It obviously hadn't affected sales but it was likely holding them back and was incredibly hard to manage.

The main protest came when I asked them to turn up for work on time! I could not believe that such a simple request met with such passionate protest. You'd think I'd asked them to sacrifice their first born child!

Oddly enough, the client actually ended up buying a finger print entry system for the office which was quite cool and said "Good Morning" when you scanned your finger print and in the interest of fair play, I happily added myself to the list of people required to use it.

As you can imagine, it caused a bit of a stir initially, but it soon settled down.

Chapter 7

The other cry I've heard many times usually happens around December time and it's generally used as a prelude to missing target!

"Nobody wants to buy"

"I would disagree" is my usual response "and in my experience, the opposite is very often the case."

I will agree that this is generally more on the B2C side rather than B2B but the fact remains the same - throughout December people are spending every spare minute buying, if anything they are in a buying frenzy (and have been since Halloween!) they are buying things they don't want or need, they are in a good mood because time off is imminent and they're going to be at home (I'd like to say 'waiting for your call' but we can't have everything our own way!)

Let me give you an example…

A while ago we were working with a call centre on a project for a regional newspaper where they were tasked with increasing their readership with new customers – similar to the Melksham project.

They usually close for the festive period but this particular year we stayed open and on the project across the Christmas/New Year break and the result was just short of an extra 200 new customers for the paper that we possibly wouldn't have got had we not stayed on it. And as usual, not being one to expect others to do something that I won't, I came in with them.

I also remember working with the team at Aquatec where the field sales team would fight over who would work during Christmas and New Year because it generally meant guaranteed sales (almost!)

The moral of the story?

December is the same as any other month, work it as hard as you would any other month and don't give up too easily

As I've probably mentioned once or twice, the

glamorous side of being a consultant means that you spend a large part of your life on the motorway and probably an equally sized part living in hotels.

Many of the consultants I've met on my travels will jump on the train and so on but being a tiny bit on the control freak side I always prefer to drive. It has meant some early mornings on occasion, but that's the choice you make.

I think probably the worst drive I've had would be driving back from Bradford to Clevedon on a Friday night. I left the clients office in Bradford at exactly 6:00pm and arrived home at 1:05am. The joys of road works and accidents on the M6 and then road closures on the M5. Not my most fun trip.

Another one that springs to mind is when Jane Thomas at the South West Contact Centre Forum sent me off to Preston for a fortnight.

As ever I'd decide to drive up, the difficulty came when the water pump on my car went on Saturday morning when I was due to drive up on the Sunday.

Two phone calls later – one to my long time friend and absolute scholar, Eddie to get the car sorted and another to Enterprise Car Rental – and Sunday afternoon I'm packing the essentials into a SEAT Ibiza.

Preston was an interesting project. We were conducting a Needs Analysis on a 600 seat call centre. Those things are always quite involved so making sure you have extensive notes is always a good idea. Knowing that my handwriting gets worse as the day goes on I always write my notes straight to the laptop.

It was here that I discovered the joys of the banana and peanut butter toasted sandwich. When they first mentioned it I wasn't convinced but always being keen to try new things I thought "What the heck" and it's actually quite nice.

They also have a McDonalds around the corner which is a bit dangerous if you're trying to avoid takeaway food – I would tell you a story about that but it might get me in trouble!

There were some interesting issues on this project, not least recruitment. When I spoke to the recruitment team and asked about attrition rates, the spreadsheet they showed me was a bit of a shock. Basically, in the previous month they had recruited 74 agents but lost 92. The analogy I gave them was to say that, in theory, if they closed the call centre today, they would still owe the job centre more people!!

In my own humble opinion, a big part of why they were losing so many new starters was because of the way the induction was delivered (which is what I put in the report I gave them). For me, the content was very much focused on the 'technical' side and not enough on 'Soft skills'.

Now all of us that have ever been through an induction of any length will fully appreciate that when you actually get out on the floor you go into a panic worrying about how much of it you'll remember etc. The difficulty is, if you don't have the 'soft skills' to hold a conversation with someone or at least the confidence to say to them "let me just check that for you" if you don't know the answer. Then you are not going to do very well at your job and are much more likely to leave!

I've said it before, if you don't support your team then you're going to have problems.

The other thing this situation caused was a kind of 'mouse wheel' affect for everyone else. The training team were only ever delivering inductions so therefore had no opportunity to develop their own skills. The recruitment team were constantly recruiting for the same role and therefore had no real opportunity to develop their own skills. The Team Leader population struggled to keep new starters engaged because they weren't staying and so found it difficult to find the time to develop those that did stay because of the constant turnover and therefore had no real opportunity....I'm sure you get the picture by now.

I will add that they took on board everything that was discussed and made some massive changes to the whole process.

I was on the Bradford project shortly after this on a similar project but my biggest problem there was that they guys I was working with were very hospitable and by the end of the week I think I'd put on several pounds!!

The biggest hurdle for that team was that the Team Leaders weren't getting any real support and that gave a knock on effect to their teams. As with the Preston project, they took on everything I said to them and changed things around.

I remember a discussion with Charlie Stockford, MD at SustainIT about whether or not sales people should be paid a commission. That was a long and very interesting conversation resulting in Charlie saying to me "Come and set up my team then". That'll teach me to have an opinion!!

Another interesting choice of focus was a client complaining that their one sales person wasn't making any sales. The conversation went something like this…

"He's not selling anything"
"OK, what's his target?"
"80 calls a day"
"What about revenue?"
"He hasn't created any"
"I understand that, but what's his target?"
"80 calls a day"
"So his only target is to make 80 calls a day?"
"Yes"

"and is he hitting that target?"
"Yes but he's not selling anything"
"You haven't asked him to, you asked him to make 80 calls a day and that's what he's doing"
"But he's supposed to sell as well"
"But you didn't ask him to, you asked him to make 80 calls a day and that's what he's doing"
"But...but..."

It was at this point that the penny started to drop and they realised the mistake they'd made.

I'll go back to my comments earlier in the book about making sure your KPIs etc are set in such a way that they benefit both the business and the agent. If you give an agent the target of making 80 calls a day then that's exactly what they're going to do. The difficulty will come when you question their performance because their response will quite rightly be "But I've hit target" and you have no defence to that.

You cannot, under any circumstances, assume that people know what is expected of them. You have to target them on exactly what you want them to do, otherwise how can you possibly question them on it if you've never actually asked them to do it.

One of the other, regular 'sticking points' is scripts and whether or not they should be used.

It's a question that has raged across the industry for many years and will probably continue to do so.

There are many different trains of thought on this subject, some for and some against.

So, should you script or not?

I've mentioned before that I have been in the industry long enough to remember when Diallers were first being used and the screen was supposed to pop up with the name of who you needed to speak to.

As I said, unfortunately, back then it didn't always work that way and you had to know what you needed to say whether it was in front of you or not. Needless to say, the whole team was pretty good at delivering the pitch without reading it!

When delivering a 'sales pitch', for the best results you need to sound confident and knowledgeable, not something that is overly easy to pull off if you're reading.

Having trained and coached many sales teams to success over the last few years I have found that not using a script when delivering the pitch works best. You don't want people sounding like they're reading.

Notice that I said 'when delivering the pitch'. What I mean by this is that, although you don't want people sounding like they're reading from a script when talking to customers, they have to learn somehow. Nobody can walk in and deliver a flawless pitch without learning it first.

What I've done in the past when training new people is to give them a script and then put a timescale on when I will take it off them. For example, they have a week's induction and then a week of training. I would test them on delivering their pitch without reading it at the end of two weeks – which should give them plenty of time.

Have a bullet-pointed version close at hand.

I'm not adverse to letting them have a bullet-pointed version close at hand, because with that they still have to fill in the gaps themselves, so you don't get the reading issue.

On the other side of the coin, you've got customer service and support teams and, as far as scripts are concerned, it's a different kettle of fish altogether.

If teams are dealing with technical issues or support there could be compliance issues, purely because they may have to ensure that they ask certain questions or get specific information.

We've all heard the 'This call may be recorded for training or compliance purposes' speech on things like payment/direct debit/cancellation instructions and it's hugely important how you deliver that 'speech' as it needs to be clear and understood.

In these instances, it's not so much about what the script says but more about how you deliver it.

From a customer's point of view, these are important facts that they need to hear, and the better the words are delivered, the more likely they are to be heard.

Customers respond better to someone who isn't reading the script – although I fully appreciate that some of these things are absolutely necessary in terms of compliance and can be quite wordy.

Taking that into consideration, I believe that a customer will respond much better to someone who obviously knows what they're doing as opposed to someone who is obviously reading the necessary questions or statements.

Alongside that, someone calling a customer service line wants to come off that call feeling better about the situation and happy that their problem will be solved. Talking to them in a non-scripted way is much more likely to achieve that than if the agent is obviously reading the questions and responses.

I would suggest that the general approach to using scripts, certainly in the sales environment, has changed somewhat over the years. With the apparent imminent death of cold calling, and the increasing numbers of people on TPS etc, that side of the industry has had to take a more consultative approach compared to the old school 'throw enough mud and some will stick' attitude of years gone by.

I had regular discussions with clients over the years telling me that they don't want their teams to use a script and I understand why. This generally comes about because the teams aren't doing as well as they'd like and so they're looking for answers.

For me, a script should be used more as a training tool and a means by which to measure performance.

Let me expand on that. As I've already said, a script is a starting point, a means by which staff can learn the ins and outs of what the business does and how to get that across to the customer – whether they're sales or customer service.

I also mentioned using it to measure performance.

Look at it like this, if everyone in the team is saying something different and your KPIs say that something is wrong, where do you start to look?

But if everyone is saying the same thing, then you at least a starting point.

Of course, you have to be confident that the

'script' they're using actually works…

The trick is to make the most of it as a learning tool but make sure your team practice, practice, practice once you have a workable script.

Confidence is key. Once they can deliver their pitch or ask a customer the right questions without the need to keep referring back to a piece of paper they will sound better, they will feel better, and so will your customers, prospective or otherwise – which in turn means more revenue.

We've no doubt all been on the receiving end of an obviously scripted call and it's never received well, so we know the downside of sticking to a script too rigidly.

On the flip side of that coin, hopefully we've also all been on the receiving end of a call delivered without reading a script and seen the obvious difference.

The worry, of course, is that people will stray too far away from the desired delivery or questions – but that's where coaching comes in.

The moral of the story is that, in my considered opinion, scripts do have their place, but more as a learning tool than something that is pure black and white fact.

On the topic of hurdles you might face and knowing my feelings on the topic, we should really give recruitment another mention.

If you want to improve attrition rates, then you may need to look more at the way that you recruit staff.

When you are starting the journey to bring in new staff, there are several things you need to consider, the first being that you want the people you recruit now to be with the business for a reasonable amount of time, otherwise you'll be constantly recruiting.

It makes sense to think about what you want the new employee or employees to do. I don't mean what their job title is. I mean what do you want them to do? Most people would call it a job description, but I always think there's more to it than that.

Think about the team dynamic.

If you're recruiting to add to an established team then you will need to think about the current team dynamic. You'll need to think about the role the new person will take within that team, what sort of personality they'll need to have.

If you want them to see this as a long-term position then you will also have to put some thought into what they might want out of it.

All too often in the past, there has been a 'bums on seats' mentality, which has done two things. It has pushed attrition rates forever upwards and it has damaged the somewhat fragile reputation of the industry.

Recruiting staff is a task that should never be taken lightly because your staff make the very backbone of your business.

What will make people stay?

Recruiting for the long term is an involved and delicate operation. Not only do you need to consider what skills and personality traits the new employee will need and what will be expected of them once they join the team, but also what will make them stay.

For sales people, the immediate answer is always money! And, yes, that will make up a good-size portion of what will interest a sales team member but, contrary to popular belief, it is not the be all and end all. All the money in the world won't make a difference if you're working in a negative and messy environment with equipment that doesn't work – although it may well soften the blow.

Look at the working environment.

Customer service teams will pay even more attention to their environment as they don't generally have the big financial rewards to rely on.

I have worked with many sales and customer service teams over the years and I can safely say that the companies that have the most long-serving team members are those that take in to consideration things outside of job descriptions.

If you want those that you employ to be committed and focused on the job you are asking them to undertake then you have many areas to consider.

Don't put too much faith in the CV.

Think about the recruitment process. Think about the interview process. I always find that a two-stage or two-person approach works well. In no small part because it then takes out any personal opinion and becomes a discussion between two professionals.

I for one never put too much faith in what I see in a CV. They are too easily manipulated.

Telephone interviews.

It will never cease to amaze me that someone recruiting for a call centre or telesales team won't, first and foremost, conduct a telephone interview. How can you even consider someone for that type of role if you firstly don't know how they cope on the telephone?

With no desire to get into a row over discrimination, what I'm talking about here is clarity. Are they clear and concise over the telephone? Can they make themselves understood by an irate customer?

If they can't, you'll frustrate your customers and the agent will not be happy in the role and will not be a long-term employee.

Staff have to feel comfortable.

For them to see the role as a long-term prospect, they have to feel comfortable, they have to feel confident, and they have to like where they work.

Give them a good remuneration package with a sensible amount of holiday allowance – long-term employee.

Good, clean environment with equipment that works – long term-employee.

Supportive managers that don't continually ask them to do things outside of their job description (although we all have to be flexible) – long-term employee.

As you can see, recruiting for the long term is far more than just a good advert and a solid job description. If you want to recruit for the long term, you have to consider what it means for an employee to be with you for the long term and what that actually entails.

And just to be really obscure before I get lost in more stories, I was once asked the question "Do you think that the weather affects agents moods?"

I'm sure we've all heard of Seasonal Affective Disorder (SAD), which basically means that some people's emotions are more susceptible to changes in the weather than others'. Oddly enough, most people's moods are affected by more everyday occurrences.

How can we deal with it from our side of the fence?

From a customer service side, being aware of how the weather can affect people, we can approach calls with that in mind and act accordingly

From the sales side of the coin, the weather can be a great way to build rapport, so in that instance it could be beneficial.

If your team is well trained, professional and motivated, then the weather should have less of an effect on performance. We can't do anything about the mood of a customer at the initial point of contact but what we can do is act in such a way that their mood doesn't affect how we deal with them or the result of their call.

On saying that, we can of course pre-empt any 'mood swings' with our teams and act accordingly. I remember working with the guys in Melksham, when one day we all turned up in the morning to a snow-covered car park and the minute I walked in I could sense the opinion about the weather and consequently their mood. My response was to send the HR Manager off to McDonald's to buy 27 breakfasts and then gave one to all the staff, which instantly improved their mood and gave us a pretty good day of sales.

I have met some real characters over the years and I've talked about some of them already and one that springs to mind whenever I have to go to London is Gemma at ReTell. I delivered several training and coaching sessions over a few months for ReTell and when we talked about voices and customer engagement Gemma stood out as one of those people with those fabulous 'sing song' voices. Having listened to lots of call recordings of her voice I remember saying to her once that "Every time I listen to your calls, I almost expect you to end the call with OK, love you, bye!"

She just smirked at me and said "Yeah...I've done that"

Then you've got the girls at Take Me Too. They're a river cruise company with an inbound sales team that I did some work with.

I remember Sasha taking me to get some lunch to a Jamaican takeaway in Gloucester.

Now you may remember that I grew up in Gloucester so knew where this place was when she told me and having sampled the delights of Jamaican cooking whilst growing up I was more than happy.

So, there we are, the lovely Sasha and me stood at the counter ordering our food and there's four young guys sniggering away at their table. Now you have to imagine the scene and what an odd couple we no doubt looked. You've got Sasha the ebony goddess and me, 6' 4" white guy in a suit ordering fried chicken with rice and peas. The giggle came for us when Sasha says

"Did you get that Stu?"
"Yeah, most of it"

At this point the sniggering stops as the boys realise that I've understood pretty much everything they've been saying!

Much laughter ensued from both sides and to their credit, they came straight over and apologised with lots of "We were just playing about" etc I should explain that at 20 years old I spent my weekends Djing at a club in Gloucester and on Saturday nights English and Patois were spoken in equal amounts, so I got used to it.

I also seem to remember a donut eating competition that I was involved in (and won by the way) that Kirsty Jones started – I believe there's video proof somewhere. In fact, when I think about it, most of the stories at Take Me Too revolve around food!!

The girls were great to work with because they really wanted some changes in the business so really dived into the stuff we did – always makes life easier when people want to improve.

Another occasion involving me and food was when I was up in Birmingham delivering a few days training and on the Friday the client says "Come on I'll take you for lunch"

I can't remember the name of it but there's a road in that part of Birmingham that is basically end to end restaurants. So we stop off at an Arabic place and being fairly game I let the client choose the food. Out comes this huge plate of all sorts of meats – the lamb was actually green! - and the client hands me a spoon and says to get stuck in. Credit where it's due, the meat was so tender a spoon was all you needed!

The funny thing was that this was mid-afternoon and I couldn't understand why everyone was stood around waiting and looking at us (we were the only ones eating) so I say to my client,

"Is something wrong?"

"No it's OK, they're just waiting to go and pray"

"Oh"

Needless to say, we finished up sharpish and got out of their way. It was definitely a first for me.

Chapter 8

I've been asked to speak at events etc many times and always really enjoy it. I've been to numerous business clubs, a boat in Gloucester Quays and even at a couple of schools.

Bristol Free School was an interesting one. I went to a breakfast event there and got talking to some of the team which later resulted in them asking me to help them organise a training day where we would give the students some sessions on presentation and communication skills and then conduct some mock interviews at the end.

Always amazes me these days that some many students have the ambition to work for themselves rather than get jobs – business is the new rock 'n' roll!!

They also asked me to be a keynote speaker which meant a lunchtime visit to the school. The difficulties started when I got stuck in bad weather on the motorway and ended up being about 15 minutes late.

I rock up to the assembly hall to be faced with a bunch of irritable teenagers who've been sat around waiting for me to arrive, to which I immediately apologise and quickly head for the teacher. Who consequently tells me she's having trouble getting the Powerpoint to 'do what it's told!'

I just look at her and say "No worries, I'll just make something up".

Not sure I've ever seen someone look so scared!

I just jump on the stage and start talking.

30 minutes later (and a Powerpoint eventually working) I take a breath and answer a few questions, so it all worked out in the end.

The teacher did say to me afterwards "How do you do that?"

"Do what?"

"Turn up late, no Powerpoint, just start talking

and not falter the whole time?"

"Oh that, it's easy if you love it!"

And I do, I remember giving a talk for Tewkesbury Business Club. I was supposed to talk for 30 minutes and while I was in full swing answering questions, giving tips and I can see one of the organisers edging towards the stage looking at his watch.

As ever, those of you that know me will not be at all surprised that once I start talking there's no stopping me!!

Young Enterprise was another great thing to be asked to get involved in. If you don't know it, basically a group of teenagers studying business, get to set up and run their own business for the academic year. My job was to mentor them.

My team were absolutely fantastic and worked incredibly hard and were rewarded by winning an award for Best Bristol Team and £500.

That was quite funny because it costs a few hundred for a team to enter and the school had

179

previously said they may not do next year because of the cost. So next morning the kids turn up to school, give the Head the cheque and politely say

"We're doing next year!"

With over 20 years in the industry consulting, training, coaching etc I apologise if I've forgotten any particular clients or projects, I promise it's not intentional.

People like Paul Hughes at Businessgen in Cardiff Bay who thought it was hilarious when I had to drive from Bristol across the bridge to Wales in a blizzard in a MG Metro!!

Or Ian Hutchinson at Mapfree Abraxas one of my first projects who I helped to organise a calling campaign for.

Or David Twemlow at Mapa Spontex when we spent our days talking about rubber gloves etc.

Or the team at Gemini Vehicle Solutions where I had two of the tyres on my car blow out on the journey up there.

And again, just to show that I'm always happy to do things above and beyond the usual, I got involved with the exhibition side of things with Cathy and the girls at Aquatec.

That was an experience I can tell you.

We've all no doubt been to an exhibition or business shows at some point and when you arrive as a delegate the stands always look great. But I can promise you, there is a massive amount of work that goes on beforehand.

Leave aside the forms you have to fill in and the health and safety checks etc. There's the fact that if there are shell scheme stands involved it's going to be a long and painful process.

I remember rocking up to Olympia in London late on a Thursday afternoon with a van loaded with two metre high pictures that needed to be fixed to the shell stand (it's a good job I'm 6' 4") and all sorts of other paraphernalia.

A couple of hours later and after much huffing and puffing from me Cathy and the girls return and say,

"That looks good"

I was a tired and probably sweaty mess by then
and unable to do much more that grunt my
agreement. To their credit, they did then drag me
off to Nando's for tea before I drove home.

One of the best shows I did with the girls was the
Food and Drink Show at UWE in Bristol. Purely
because at the end of it, some of the other
exhibitors were giving away their wares so the
girls and I left with bags of cakes, bread, beer etc.

One of the worst we did was the Over 50's Show
at Alexandra Palace when very few people
actually visited the show and we spent two days
talking to the other exhibitors!!

We also did lots of garden centres at weekends
which tended to be really great or absolutely dire.
My Son Jack used to love visiting the girls at the
garden centre on a weekend to see how they were
getting on.

One of the things I learnt right at the start of my
consulting career is that you cannot be 'all things
to all men' and you shouldn't try. It's far better to

work out what you're good at and then do it very well.

What I also learnt was to build relationships with industry experts and then when you get asked a question that you don't have the answer to you have an expert to call upon.

It does two things

1. It doesn't pull your focus away from what you should be doing and
2. It gets your client the information they need.

Which in turn makes you look like the expert you are supposed to be.

The other thing (and I think I've mentioned this already) is that you should never stop learning. I still regularly read books on sales, telesales, call centres etc

What follows is some words of wisdom from some of the people I personally call upon when I don't have the answer…

OK, let's start with recruitment (we all know I'm

not a fan so let's get it out of the way). It's at this point that I'm going to do what I always do when it comes to recruitment and pass the buck to Natalie Rosato, MD at Rosato Recruitment, and she came up with 5 tips for recruiting in a call centre...

"I have always remembered a brilliant piece of advice I was given when I started in recruitment many years ago. It was "the harder the interview process, the bigger the candidates desire for the role will be" and I feel this perfectly sums up the biggest pitfall most contact centres fall in to when recruiting. Most centres are recruiting multiple candidates simultaneously and the fear and desperation to fill the quota usually shines through in their interview process. The aim of this advice is to get you to not fall in to the trap of the "easy hire" and take a little extra time, think outside the box and watch your retention figures rise and rise.

Here are my top five hints to help you recruit successfully:

1) Calibre of candidate

Too many centres will only consider candidates with experience. Most centres are entry level roles and I would choose the candidate with no experience over the candidate who has done three-month stints at every other centre in the vicinity, every single time. The loyalty and determination you will receive from a candidate given a break can never be equaled. Forget CVs, you are hiring on personality, resilience and desire, a CV will never show you those qualities, hold an assessment day, look beyond experience and hire a group who not only have skill but work together, motivate and instil success in each other, your overall results will improve dramatically.

2) Assessment days

Good sales people can promise the world in a 15-minute interview, it's a little harder to maintain the façade for a whole day. It may feel laborious taking a full day out of your schedule however, if run well, this one day will produce better results than lots of individual interviews making the day a much more efficient use of your time. Make sure each exercise is relevant to the role they are applying for. Put them in real life situations to see how they handle things in the moment. Being able to handle difficult or uncomfortable conversations is such an appropriate skill that you will never find evidence of on a CV. If you are hiring a group of people, you want that group to have the ability to work cohesively, an assessment day gives you the perfect opportunity to observe the candidates interacting with each other. Getting a team to work well involves more than one or two individuals who are exceptional. Hiring teams that work well together will stop the revolving door of new starters. I would rather have a group of above average sales people than a group with one or two superstars.

3) B2B v B2C

Forget the myth that experienced B2C candidates are not polished or professional enough for a B2B environment. I have always found B2C candidates have far more resilience. They are used to a much less professional response to a cold call, they are well versed at building relationships quickly and getting past gate keepers and clients who don't realise there is this untapped pool of potential, really are missing out on so many great candidates. Take the "door to door" sales people, who work commission only and get wet when it rains. Offer them a seat, a basic salary and a roof should it rain and be amazed at the results they can produce. These are the guys who, in my opinion, have the strongest work ethic, they will keep knocking those doors until they make a sale, give them a phone and a decent working environment and they will become your top earners. (plus, when you tell them they will be working 9am – 5pm Monday to Friday instead of evenings and weekends, they will think they have hit the jackpot!)

4) Be Honest

Never oversell the role. Sales can be tough, there are days when you need pure resilience and determination to keep going and if the candidates are not prepared for this, their first tough day can result in them giving up. Don't promise ridiculous OTE's if they are unachievable as it will just demotivate your staff. Psychologically, candidates who have been told their OTE is £25,000 will be happier when they achieve £30,000 than candidates who have been told their OTE is £40,000 and they achieve £35,000. People are very much more motivated when they feel a sense of over achievement. Tell the truth, if the product or market you are in is saturated and is a tough sell, tell them from the start, the ones who choose to move forward with the role will have had their expectations managed from the start and will not be put off by a bad day.

5) Manage your own expectations

There is no such thing as 'the perfect candidate' (I wish there was!) so be realistic. If the role you are offering is a minimum wage role, don't be disappointed that you have not found the next Bill Gates in your latest round of recruitment. Similarly, don't expect contact centre work to be for everyone, if you hire ten people, chances are, all ten will not complete training but that's OK and if you were expecting it, it is easier to take in your stride. I have always worked on a rule of thumb that 2 out of 3 new starters will stick. Similarly, not everyone making it through the process should be something you address on the first day of training. A group all starting a new job on the same day will quickly build a camaraderie. When one leaves, the whole group can quickly become unstable so address this on the first day of training and avoid the domino effect.

Truthfully, there is no hard and fast rule or golden secret to successfully recruiting in a call centre however using these tips will hopefully help, I know they have helped me".

You can contact Natalie on 01633 749 640 or natalie@rosato-recruitment.com

Now you can see why I've had her helping me with mine and my clients recruitment for many years!

Next I thought about call recording, it's much bigger now than it was when I first started, so again I place you in the hands of an expert, namely Everton Stuart, MD at Vidicode.

I asked Everton what impact call recording has on business.

In the 80's and 90's call recording was a dark art...which came with high cost, great difficult to find data and relatively poor technical support and resilience.

This meant that it was only used by those businesses that needed it for regulations, mainly big banks, who would use it to keep a check on insider trading and other potential expensive litigious issues.

Fast forward 30 years, and you would be hard pressed to find any company that is conducting anything via a telephone and doesn't have a call recorder in place or is not in the process of considering a call recording solution. Be it for a mobile, cloud or onsite solution. Call recording has become big business and is now almost a commodity item and a must for most businesses. The big question now for companies is not about whether they should record calls, but focus is about security, compliance and integration API's with recording solutions.

In the coming months and years, focus will be centered around voice analytics as users will need a simple way to access, process and find calls with particular phrases that are of interest to them from multiple months or years of recordings that they may be forced to keep for legislative or other means.

Call recording in its most simple non – compliant format, can help companies move from paper based systems to electronic systems, where contracts are done verbally rather than waiting 3 weeks for signed PO's and contracts. A telesales person can now close a deal over the phone, with paper work sent via email or in the post to confirm what has been agreed. One company grew from 10 to 100 employees in 2 years after implementing a similar system for cheaper energy sales.

For regulated firms, PCI DSS – applies if they take card payments over the phone, MiFIDII for Financial (FCA) Firms and the 2018 GDPR data protection regulations means that customers must invest in the "right" technology not just the "free" or cheapest ones that may have been provided as part of a unified offering.

This has created specialist technologists and software companies to assist with all these changes, which help companies to improve and win more business by staying focused on their core business functions.

If nothing else call recording and speech analytics is a great way to cut time wasting and keep disputes and business uncertainties down to a minimum.

Any business that wants to work smarter should start by looking at a call recording system to help improve their services and processes.

These 3 questions apply to all industries and a good call recording solution can help answer and improve your business by answering these questions.

1.How many missed calls came into your business in the past day, week or month?

2.How do your customers feel about the service they received over the phone by your staff / agents?

3.How can you improve your customers experience with your business when speaking to agents or staff members?"

If that's prompted some questions for you, call Everton on 07957 402 645

One of the things that lots of us working in the industry are prone to is gaining a couple of extra pounds around the middle, purely because we sit down all day, get stuck eating at ours desks and so on.

With that in mind I thought I'd ask my buddy Sarah Dineen at Fit2Drop what she had to say about it.

"We all know that as a human race our lives are more sedentary now than ever. We have machines that do jobs we used to physically do ourselves such as washing and dishes. We have motorised vehicles that transport us everywhere rather than walking and our jobs are less physical as well, particularly when you work in a call centre environment.

This doesn't mean we have to accept the outcome: which can lead to increased risk of terminal illnesses, skeletal issues and shorter life expectancy. YOU can make positive and healthy changes for yourself to counteract the effects of being sedentary for a large portion of the day. Just because you are plugged in doesn't mean you don't need to move, why not kick your chair away and stand for 10 Minutes then sit for 10 minutes alternatively? This will get the blood flowing to your large global muscles and in turn make your more alert too, leading to better efficiency?

In fact go one better and request a standing desk or a gym-ball to sit to help increase your core strength. There are stretches you can do at your desk as well, ones to help mobilise and strengthen your neck and shoulders. Sit tall and lift your arms up in line with your shoulders then draw your elbow back keeping it high and retract your shoulder blades, alternate sides. You can also do head rolls, dropping your ear to one side and then chin to your chest to help reduce postural changes such as kyphosis which can lead to chronic pain in your upper back.

Lastly look at your nutrition - do you make healthy choices? Do you prepare your lunches and snacks for the day or rely on vending machines to keep you fuelled? Did you know on average each person based in a desk job consumes an extra 100,000 calories per year from snacks alone? That could lead to weight gain as much as 2 stone if the snacks you choose are unhealthy ones.....this study has been carried out in the US, but makes you think now about what you fuel your body with. Plus eating sugar and high processed food leads to energy spikes and lows as well.

You can make positive small changes like bring in fresh fruit, nuts, seeds and vegetables if you really can't go without your snacks. Prepare your lunch the night before, so it's home made therefore you know exactly what has gone into it and aren't reaching for something quick and unhealthy. In the long term your body will thank you for moving more, eating better and putting your health first. Just because you sit down for your job, doesn't mean you can't be healthy".

So, there you have it, no excuses anymore and if you want to ask Sarah yourself drop her an email on sarah@fit2drop.com

As he's been up and down the country with me, I thought it only fair to let Steve Drew have a little say, so I'll take you back to when somebody asked him about coaching…

I already coach. Why isn't my team improving?

The effect of NOT coaching effectively

Often the difficulty here is that your staff will already feel demotivated and frustrated at not being able to hit what feel like unrealistic goals – they then receive additional pressure from above to be doing more without the appropriate support and challenge.

The result? No improvement and, in some cases, a further drop in morale and performance – and yes, the cycle becomes more tense.

It's worth noting that absenteeism alone costs companies 8.4 days on average per year, which equates to £659 per employee, according to a recent Management Report by the CIPD.

Break the cycle

Time is often a reason (excuse) for not coaching. Yet, in most case studies, the most significant drains on time for a leader or coach are the unnecessary questions and problem solving presented by those they could and should be coaching.

Typically, a good coaching session will leave the coachee feeling like they have been involved and they will identify things that they want to be better at, whilst being guided by the coach. They will feel better able to find and resolve issues themselves.

This collaborative approach can both support and challenge the individual to actually want to be better at what they do, rather than feel they 'have to'.

What tools are needed for a good coaching session?

A simple coaching structure, good questioning techniques and a clear understanding of what the end result looks like will help motivate the coachee to see how they can make a difference without being told, and will give the coach vital confidence in their approach, bringing both consistency to the process and the value back to coaching.

Coaching Process

1. Introduction

Make sure there is good signposting at the outset of what is expected from both parties, and paint the picture of the end result.

2. Review the improvement area together

Be it listening to a recorded call, looking at the quality of data input or considering missed sales opportunities, looking at the challenge together

gives you both the chance to discuss and compare both sets of findings.

3. Good notes

Your notes can easily be placed into sections or headings of "what got your attention" "Specific example" "What was the impact?" and this leads you nicely into effective questioning.

4. Summarising

Using your notes, asking simple open and signposting questions, have the coachee tell you what they thought they did well. It's important that you have the coachee summarise and note down those areas. Then do the same for the areas they've identified they could/should improve on – again with the coachee to summarise to you and then note down.

5. Overall summary

Reminding the staff member that they have identified positive and development areas, have them read back the summaries they have made to reinforce their own learning.

6. How?

The vital element here is to have the staff member explain how they're going to make any agreed changes. "I will remember" is never good enough, because they simply won't. It's often a good idea to paint the picture of a busy day and have them specifically describe to you what they will do that's going to be different.

What will be the result?

Through having effective engagement and meaningful conversations, you will have a more motivated mindset from your teams, as well as from the team leader, coach or advisor. They will all have a feeling of development, sense of achievement and will place a much greater value on the activity of coaching.

The impact to you and your business will be improvement in areas such as customer contact, sales conversion, quality and both customer and staff retention, ensuring stronger revenue streams and reduced operational spend in a time when service and cost are the key to success.

As I mentioned before, I have no doubt that I've missed out lots of people and clients whilst writing this book and to you I apologise, there have been quite a few over the years and I'm not getting any younger!!

Running any kind of phone based operations is a minefield, it's a day to day battle of spinning plates and fighting fires and if I'm completely honest, I've loved every minute of it!

Starting out on my own was both scary and exciting, it's been an absolute roller coaster ride of highs and lows, I've been involved in some fantastic projects and I've been involved in some 'interesting' ones. I've spent days on motorways and in hotels and sat up late at night writing proposals and training sessions (there's that glamour again!)

I've had times when clients didn't pay me and caused me a few headaches. Which isn't very funny I can promise you. But a bit of hard work and some negotiation and I always seemed to pull something out of the depths of defeat.

In fact, let me give you a couple of examples to

show you what I mean.

I remember one occasion while I was waiting for a payment to come in when we had to raid the penny jar to buy a pint of milk. Ridiculous as it was, the payment came in next day!

Or another time when I was working away and therefore staying in a hotel but I couldn't really afford to eat in the restaurant as you normally would so I took three days worth of 'packed lunch' food with me so that I could eat – thankfully, I got paid a couple of days later.

Like I said, consulting is such a glamorous life!

To add to that, I've had some laughs and made some great friends along the way and the whole thing has been a massive adventure. An adventure that has allowed me to write two books (when I finish this one) numerous articles and speak at events.

If reading this book gives you just one little snippet that helps you then I'm happy. Working in the industry is hard work, but can be loads of fun.

Recently, I took on the role of Head of Global Training & Development and built from scratch a complete training and coaching program for a sales team that's based in offices all over the world.

Let me push that point home for you. I remember flying to Hong Kong to deliver a week long induction. Now I'm sure you're all thinking "that sounds great" and yes it does sounds great. But let me put it into perspective for you.

Flying to Hong Kong takes about 13 hours and although the airport is air conditioned, when the doors open to the outside world, it feels like someone has turned a hair dryer on you at full speed on the highest heat level such is the humidity.

Taking a taxi is an event all in itself, most of them look like they would fall apart in a strong wind with wires etc all over the dashboard and drivers that spend most of the journey talking to someone else on the phone. On the upside, they are also generally very accommodating in terms of help with cases etc.

Hospitality in the hotels is really good, very helpful and breakfast is an adventure.

You basically rock up to the dinning room and you are faced with a long table containing everything from salad to pastries to eggs and bacon and you just grab a plate and tuck in!

With the Chinese not be known for their height and me being a little on the tall side, walking from the hotel to the office was like being in Gulliver's Travels. Added to the fact that you had to walk through the 'red light' district to get to the office walking back to the hotel at the end of the day was always interesting.

So, I arrive in Hong Kong and grab a taxi to the hotel and get myself organised (little tip, try not to fall asleep in the afternoon, it really doesn't help!).

When I'm away I usually Skype my Son Jack and it was quite funny to be talking to him and say "I'm going to bed now mate" when he's on his way home from school (gotta love a seven hour time difference)

The induction I was delivering was being to delivered to several offices at the same time so although I was in the Hong Kong office with some of the team, we also had people on video conference in Dubai, Cape Town, Jo'burg and London and trying to match everyone up and deliver all the content meant 12 hour days for yours truly.

Jet lag hit me on Wednesday which made for an interesting day and on Thursday the CEO walked passed the training room while we were about to break for lunch and said "You OK Stu, you look tired?" I suspect that the look on my face prompted the next comment which was "Come on, I'll take you to lunch".

The boys and girls on the induction tell me that I nailed it but I assure you, trying to keep everyone interested and involved when you're dealing with 4 different times zones and 80% of the delegates not in the room.

It's a sign of the times I guess that more and more training and coaching is conducted remotely and there's two things that spring to mind.

Firstly, I'm convinced that we will never completely remove face to face (classroom) training and secondly, delivering training etc over video conferencing changes the way you deliver.

Controlling the 'room' becomes a different task altogether. You have to be much more aware of holding delegates attention, you have to slow down when you talk, you have to finds ways to get delegates much more involved than you perhaps normally would.

Any trainer will agree that keeping the delegates focused is one of the most important tasks in any session, but when you have so many other possible disruptions (that you have no control over) the issue is increased ten fold.

When you deliver training over video (such as Skype etc) you have to encourage delegate input twice as much as you would in a classroom session.

In my time in the role, I delivered numerous sessions over video and it really does change the way you approach sessions. Add in to the mix that you may have to deal with different cultures and different levels of ability in spoken English, it takes a certain level of skill to get it right. It takes practice but stick with it, it may change the way you deliver training but it creates a different realm for jokes.

We all know that I love a good story, so let me add a video conference story in to show, yet again, that I am by no means infallible.

I'm in London, sat on a video call to the global sales force, not presenting, just partaking and in the midst of it all, young Matt (who's elsewhere meeting a client on behalf of one of the guys in Dubai) calls my mobile to tell me that the client has phoned to say they are running late by about an hour.

I knew he was doing this so when he called I thought I'd better answer, so I click off the camera so as not to seem rude and answer the call.

The conversation goes something like this...

"Hi Stu, the guy has just called me to say he'll be about and hour late"

"Damn, OK, well at least he's still coming. You OK to wait around for him?"

"Yeah, I'm in Woolwich so not great but it's fine I'll wait"

So I jokingly say

"Good lad, just find a quite corner and play by yourself for an hour"

Take that how you will. Matt just laughed and said "It's fine I'll occupy myself with something"

I giggle and cut off the call, then I hear "Stu", it's Tom Bland head of the Jo'burg office.

Still not catching on I say "Yes mate?"

"Your mic is still on"

I just paused for a second and then burst out laughing with a "Thanks Tom"

In case you hadn't worked out where I went wrong, I had just been heard by the global sales force telling Matt to go play with himself for an hour!

Note to self, if you're not presenting on the call, turn off your mic!

As I said, not infallible but when you're training audiences across the globe the allowance for 'hiccups' increases.

It's also quite an odd feeling when you're speaking to people across the world from a London office and trying to remember where they are and if you say good morning or afternoon!

When all is said and done, I've had some laughs and made some great friends along the way and the whole thing has been a massive adventure.

Forgive me for repeating myself, but I just want to once again, say a massive thank you to all of you that have been with me on this journey, to all those that have endured being trained by me I hope some of it was useful and to those that I will train in the future...you have been warned, I have not learned my trade in an exam room, what I teach comes from experience and by finding what works and passing it on.

I've had some fantastic comments and feedback from the people I have trained but if I can leave you with one piece of advice it's this.

Training isn't enough, you actually have to act on it and put into action the things you are taught. Otherwise it's pointless.

"Stuart is an engaging and energetic trainer. He is extremely focused and driven which ensures his training sessions are memorable".

"During his training sessions, I have experienced a new and refreshed way of being trained, with an unrivalled articulation if situations into real-life examples. It feels like second nature to learn with Stu".

"Stuart is extremely professional and has transformed our telesales unit into a vibrant, energetic and profitable proportion of our business."

"Everything was perfect. I have never enjoyed training as much as I enjoyed receiving training from Stuart."

"I was extremely impressed with how easy it was to work with him and how passionate he was about the whole course."

"Stuart is passionate, hard working and fun at the same time. He is a pleasure to deal with! Definitely deserves to win."

"Stuart knows his industry inside out, and has not only the industry knowledge, but people skills to impart his knowledge and have a positive impact on those he is working with and also training."

"His knowledge of all aspects of Call Centre operations is immense, and he is an excellent trainer and coach and team leader."

"Absolutely fantastic leader in his field."

"He knows how to get the best out of contact centre teams – with humour, insight and leadership."

.

29689216R00124

Printed in Great
Britain
by Amazon